IN SEARCH OF ҖECOVERY

CHRISTOPHER CVIIĆ
AND PETER SANFEY

In Search of the Balkan Recovery

The Political and Economic Reemergence of South-Eastern Europe

HURST & COMPANY, LONDON

First published in the United Kingdom in 2010 by
C. Hurst & Co. (Publishers) Ltd.,
41 Great Russell Street, London, WC1B 3PL
© Christopher Cviić and Peter Sanfey 2010
All rights reserved.
Printed in India

The right of Christopher Cviić and Peter Sanfey to be identified
as the authors of this publication is asserted by them in accordance
with the Copyright, Designs and Patents Act, 1988.

A Cataloguing-in-Publication data record for this book
is available from the British Library.

ISBNs: 978-1-84904-069-3 *clothbound*
 978-1-84904-070-9 *paperback*

www.hurstpub.co.uk

This book is printed using paper from registered sustainable
and managed sources.

CONTENTS

ACKNOWLEDGEMENTS

This book arose from many years of collaboration on South-Eastern Europe as colleagues within the Office of the Chief Economist at the European Bank for Reconstruction and Development (EBRD). We are grateful to the Chief Economists, Willem Buiter (2000–05) and Erik Berglof (2006–present) for their support over the years, as well as to numerous other colleagues within the EBRD who have enriched our understanding of this region. Frank Ryan and his colleagues in the EBRD's Business Information Centre were particularly helpful in providing data and other materials.

A number of people provided useful comments on parts or all of the manuscript. We thank Marko Atanasovsky, Chris Beauman, Branko Caratan, Simon Commander, Olivier Descamps, Ivo Germann, Roland Jovanović, Thomas Mirow (President of the EBRD), Zlatko Nikoloski, Craig Otter, and Gabriel Partos for very helpful suggestions and corrections. We are also grateful to an anonymous reviewer who provided extensive and highly constructive suggestions for extending and improving the text. Of course we remain responsible for any errors or other shortcomings. We would also like to thank Michael Dwyer and his colleagues at Hurst & Co. Publishers for their careful production of this book.

Finally, we thank our families, Celia, Stephen and Antonia Cviić and Jelena and Gregor Sanfey, for their support and patience. The book is dedicated to them.

FOREWORD

Willem Buiter

Chris Cviić and Peter Sanfey have written a remarkable book on the political and economic developments that have shaped the former Communist countries of South-Eastern Europe (aka 'the Balkans') since the fall of the Berlin Wall. It is short, readable and full of insights. The authors—I was privileged to work with both of them at the European Bank for Reconstruction and Development during the period 2000–2005— bring unrivalled knowledge and understanding of the region to this project.

Those who have lost track of the region after peace broke out in Bosnia and Herzegovina following the Dayton Agreement of 1995, or after Slobodan Milošević resigned the presidency of the Federal Republic of Yugoslavia in 2000, will be surprised to read of the progress made even in Bosnia and Herzegovina and in Kosovo (the countries most tragically afflicted by armed conflict, mass murder and ethnic cleansing), and in Serbia, which until the end of 2000 suffered under a repressive and corrupt political regime and destructive economic policies.

When I reached the end of the book, I had gained a much better understanding of the remarkable achievements of the people of the region: peace despite a history of centuries of internecine conflict; bright prospects for future economic growth (despite the north-Atlantic financial crisis and the global economic downturn); stronger institutional foundations for democracy and the rule of law; three countries (Slovenia, Bulgaria and Romania) already in the EU, two more queuing up (Croatia and Macedonia) and a realistic prospect of membership for all the others (Albania, Bosnia and Herzegovina, Serbia, Montenegro and Kosovo). I also achieved a better appreciation of the challenges that still remain, including the continuing reality that there often appears to be a 'region' only in the strict geographical sense of the word. The absence of any strong sense of common regional identity is underlined by the countries' EU accession strategies: every country looks severally to Brussels—there is no substantive regional EU accession approach. The Brussels-made rules of the accession game encourage such continued 'balkanisation', of course.

Whether your tastes run to history and politics, to macroeconomic stabilisation under extreme conditions or to structural reform following the collapse of a range of varieties of communism, you should read this book and be instructed and entertained in the process.

1

INTRODUCTION

In recent years, South-eastern Europe, or 'the Balkans' as it is still sometimes referred to, has made fewer appearances in the headlines, compared to the 1990s when it was rarely out of the news. The old adage that 'no news is good news' may be appropriate in this case. When people in the west think of this region, often what comes to mind first are the images of the wars and conflicts of the 1990s. The dramatic arrest in July 2008 of the former Bosnian Serb leader, Radovan Karadžić, provoked a re-showing of archive footage from the early 1990s and no doubt stirred up for many people, memories that had lain dormant for some time. But there is another story to tell—one of a region that has grown strongly in economic terms, attracting record flows of investment and building deep and long-lasting links with its neighbours and the outside world. These trends are less newsworthy, but they are already affecting profoundly the lives of ordinary people in the region, and they will shape future developments in the coming decades.

Why write a new book on the Balkans? There are a number of reasons. First, we believe it is important to provide a fresh perspective on recent history in South-Eastern Europe. In essence, our argument is that the past two decades have seen a gradual but irreversible shift from conflict to cooperation,

1

not just at the diplomatic and state level but also, and argu-ably more importantly, at the level of private individuals and businesses. To understand how this shift has taken place requires an analysis of both the political upheavals that have taken place over this period, and the economic forces that are currently driving the region's progress. Many books have been written about South-Eastern Europe, but few writers have looked at the interactions of economic and political interests and how these have shaped developments and prospects.

A second reason for writing this book is that developments in the region still have the potential to affect the west. South-Eastern Europe is an area of important strategic interest, and the European Union (EU) in particular has a vital stake in helping to ensure that it remains stable and becomes increas-ingly prosperous. Other major players such as the United States and Russia also have strong commercial interests in South-Eastern Europe. After a difficult period in the 1990s, the international community has come to a better understand-ing of the problems and is now playing a much more con-structive role.

Third, the region is still widely misunderstood and suffers from a severe image problem. Ever since the phrases 'The Balkan Wars' and 'Balkanisation' entered into common dis-course, people think of South-Eastern Europe as a hotbed of constant fighting, ethnic tensions and overall instability. This is hardly surprising given what happened in the 1990s. But most people, including the investor community, are favoura-bly surprised when they find out more, or even visit the region. Our hope is that, in the future, visitors and investors will be less surprised and more ready to see for themselves how much progress has been made over the past decade or so and how much potential exists for further catch-up.

This theme of potential and opportunity runs throughout the book and provides the fourth reason for embarking on this project. It often surprises people when they learn that average (weighted) economic growth in the region has exceeded that of the 'EU-8' (former communist countries that joined the EU in 2004) almost every year since 2001, and far exceeds recent growth in the 'Eurozone'. Progress in economic reform has also gone faster in recent years, in some cases (such as Bulgaria and Romania) driven by the need to adopt the EU's *acquis communautaire*. However, there is still a long way to go to catch up with standards of living not only in the 'old' EU but also in the 2004 intake. Our view is that the conditions are in place for further catch-up, but important risks remain.

As of end-2009, the region is suffering in terms of the global economic crisis, and virtually all countries are now in a recession. Nevertheless, it is well placed to take advantage of the global recovery—whenever that might occur. The possibility of instability and even conflict in the future is low, but it cannot be entirely discounted. The best approach, in our view, is to be realistic about the risks, balancing well-founded optimism about the region's bright future with a recognition that there are still important unresolved issues, notably concerning Kosovo and the aftermath of its declaration of independence in early 2008, to which Serbia is implacably opposed. However, one should not exaggerate the risks. In particular, the possibility that the region will once again become embroiled in the kind of turmoil experienced in the 1990s is, we believe, remote. More localised trouble, however, cannot be ruled out.

Finally, a note about what we mean by 'South-Eastern Europe'. Our book is fundamentally a story of transition, and therefore we focus on that part of South-Eastern Europe that has been engaged over the past two decades in the process—still unfinished—of transition from socialism to democracy and the market economy. That means Albania, Bulgaria, Romania and the former Yugoslavia (although mostly excluding Slovenia, which has from the start—not least because of its close proximity to its western neighbours Austria and Italy—followed a different path). We exclude countries such as Greece, Cyprus and Turkey, which had since the Second World War been developing under a different political and socio-economic system, although they have an important influence mainly through trade and investment links.

It is not our intention to pretend that these countries constitute a coherent region with a similar outlook and development path. Clearly, Bulgaria and Romania, which joined the EU in January 2007, and Croatia which is well on the way to membership, are more advanced in their transition than the other countries. Nevertheless, all countries under consideration have taken part in common regional initiatives (such as the Stability Pact for South East Europe) and even these advanced countries still face significant challenges to reach the standards of the most advanced market economies.

Outline of the book

Chapter II examines the upheavals in the region following the collapse of the Berlin Wall in late-1989. The chapter focuses on the break-up of Yugoslavia and the subsequent conflicts within and among the successor states, culminating in the Dayton Peace Accords in December 1995. It also analyses developments in Albania, Bulgaria and Romania over this period, as these countries embarked on their own transition. Overall, the chapter demonstrates why the whole transition process was slow to start in South-Eastern Europe, because economic reforms were sidelined by war and turmoil.

The mid-1990s appeared to be a turning point for the region, but the second half of that decade was marked by further convulsions. Chapter III outlines the reasons for the further setbacks and crises, with a focus on the Kosovo conflict of 1999 and the subsequent changes in the following decade, particularly in Croatia and Serbia. By 2008, the region has become much more stable but the political evolution has not been completely smooth. The chapter concludes with a discussion of Kosovo's declaration of independence in early-2008 and its implications for the region.

Chapter IV examines critically the role of the international community throughout the past twenty years in South-Eastern

INTRODUCTION

Europe. The chapter contrasts the dithering of the 1990s in the face of a collapsing Yugoslavia with the more constructive role played by international actors in the following decade. The fruits of this new approach have become apparent through the increased stability and cooperation in the region and the progress towards European Union integration, with Bulgaria and Romania having successfully joined the EU in 2007.

The analysis then turns to an evaluation of the region's economic evolution. Chapter V assesses economic and reform developments over the whole period. It outlines the progress made over the past two decades, the difficulties and reversals that the region has faced, and the current state of reform and transition. The path of transition has been particularly uneven in this part of the world, and the effects on people's lives have been even more traumatic than in other parts of the former communist bloc, notably Central Europe and the Baltic states. Nevertheless, there is still an encouraging momentum towards further institutional and economic development.

Although South-Eastern Europe has been adversely affected by the global crisis in 2008–09, it remains a region with potential to resume rapid growth over the medium-term. But how likely is it that this potential can be achieved, and what are the main risks? We analyse these questions in Chapter VI, and come up with an assessment of future prospects that is both optimistic and realistic. Long-term growth will require careful macroeconomic management of the economy and further improvements to the business environment and to policies that promote trade and investment and strengthen the quality of human capital.

Chapter VII concludes with a concise summary of the effects of the crisis on the region, and an explanation of why this does not fundamentally affect our positive conclusion about the long-term prospects for the region.

2

POLITICAL EVOLUTION AND UPHEAVAL
FROM WORLD WAR II TO THE MID-1990s

The Cold War corset

One of the most important consequences for South-eastern Europe of the break-up of the Soviet bloc, symbolised by the collapse of the Berlin Wall in November 1989, was the bursting of the tight Cold War corset that had enveloped the region for four decades after 1945. In October 1944, Winston Churchill and Joseph Stalin had reached in Moscow an informal understanding, expressed in percentages, over the division of the spheres of interest. Under the Moscow formula, Bulgaria and Romania came into the Soviet sphere of influence. Greece stayed in the Western Powers' sphere. Hungary and Yugoslavia were to be shared on a 50:50 basis, but the Soviet Union prevailed in both (as well as in Albania, which had not been discussed in Moscow). However, in 1948 it began to look as if the post-1945 *de facto* division of South-Eastern Europe might be de-stabilised.

The main reason was the expulsion of the Communist Party of Yugoslavia (KPJ) on 28 June 1948 from the Information Bureau of the Communist and Workers' Parties (or *Cominform*, as it had become popularly known in the West), a Soviet-controlled body set up in 1947 and composed of the

Communist parties of Eastern and Southern Europe and two from Western Europe. That development caused a world sensation, while to Communists everywhere it came as a shock. Until then, the Yugoslav Communist Party had, because of its successful wartime guerrilla struggle and its post-war ideological radicalism, been admired within the world Communist movement as one of the most glamorous. Its high standing was reflected in the fact that the Cominform's seat was in Belgrade. Yet, now the official Cominform communiqué was accusing the Yugoslav comrades of pursuing an 'incorrect line on the main issues of home and foreign policy'.

Balkan options

It was indeed true that under its charismatic leader, Josip Broz Tito, the Yugoslav Communist regime had in 1945 (unsuccessfully) challenged the Western Allies by an aggressive regional policy. Yugoslavia had laid a territorial claim to a part of Austria, then under 'four-Power' military occupation, as well as to (British-and US-occupied) Trieste. In the south, Tito and Georgi Dimitrov, who had from 1935 to 1943 been head of the Communist International (*Comintern*) in Moscow and had in 1945 returned to his native Bulgaria, planned to set up a Balkan Federation that was also to include Greece. It had been assumed in the West that all that was happening at the instigation of Moscow. The reality was more complex and much of the region's recent history was reflected in this project. The Comintern and the Communist parties working under its direction in the region did indeed between the two world wars advocate the setting up of a Balkan Federation in the place of Yugoslavia and the surrounding Balkan national states. The reason for Communist hostility towards the then Yugoslavia was that, since its setting up in 1918 (under the name of the Kingdom of the Serbs, Croats and Slovenes), it had—together with Romania—been a pillar of the British and French-backed *cordon sanitaire*, a barrier to the spread of influence both of Germany from the west and the Bolsheviks from the east.

The idea of a Balkan Federation was popular in Bulgaria where there was widespread resentment over the loss, at the end of the First World War (in which Bulgaria had ended up on the losing side), to Yugoslavia of the bulk of Macedonia, which the Bulgarians regarded as their land. To the Bulgarians, the possibility of reopening the Macedonian issue via the idea of a Balkan Federation was attractive. For the Bulgarian Communist Party (BKP), this represented a good tactic. Unlike in the historically strongly anti–Russian Romania, there was in Bulgaria (especially among the peasants and the less educated) a strong pro-Russian sentiment, dating back to Bulgaria's liberation from Ottoman rule in the 1877–78 Russo-Turkish war. The idea of a Balkan Federation was also popular in Yugoslav Macedonia and helped gain the Communists a lot of support there. Officially designated as 'Southern Serbia' after 1918, Macedonia had been exposed to a policy of systematic 'Serbianisation'. One of the features of this policy was its state-sponsored colonisation by ethnic Serbs from other parts of Yugoslavia. Not surprisingly, when in April 1941, following Yugoslavia's dismemberment, Macedonia was annexed to Bulgaria, the majority of the local population initially welcomed the annexation.

The end of the Yugoslav state in 1941 was also welcomed in the province of Kosovo (or in Albanian, Kosova). Its ethnic Albanian majority was, together with the Macedonians, the worst treated national group in Yugoslavia. After its dismemberment, Kosovo, together with a part of western Macedonia and an area on the eastern border of Montenegro, was incorporated by the Axis powers into a new Greater Albania under Italian tutelage. This removed from the Albanians in Albania, Kosovo and Macedonia any strong national motive for resistance against the Axis powers. The Communists were a small political force among the Albanians till mid-1943 when it began to look as if Italy was going to be knocked out of the war. The still rather weak Communists tried to negotiate a common front with the much stronger nationalist group called the Balli Kombëtar (BK). A joint document, signed in

August 1943, included a demand for self-determination in Kosovo—a *conditio sine qua non* for every Albanian nationalist. But that was unacceptable to the Albanian Communist Party's influential Yugoslav mentors. Enver Hoxha, the Albanian Communist leader, was forced to back down and break with the nationalists. The rapid intervention of the Germans after the capitulation of Italy in September 1943 was actively or passively supported by the BK and led to the wiping out of the Communist-led partisan units in the centre and north of Albania. However, by the spring of 1944, the situation had changed again. The destruction spread by the Germans and the BK had stimulated recruitment for the pro-Communist partisans who rapidly eclipsed the BK and mustered a small army to strike back in the centre and the north.

In the autumn of 1944, Enver Hoxha set up a government completely dominated by the Communist Party of Albania (PKS). The Communist Party of Yugoslavia caused friction by its attempt to make the Albanian Party into a subordinate party, but Hoxha, with his army behind him, was too powerful at the moment of victory to be overthrown. However, the Yugoslavs had the support of the second strong man in the Albanian Communist Party, Koçi Xoxe, who had sided with them at the time of the August 1943 agreement. The struggle for the control of the PKS abated for a while as the Albanian Communists found themselves obliged to accept not only the dominance of Tito-led Yugoslavia but also the full integration of Kosovo into Yugoslavia, imposed in the spring of 1945. With Yugoslavia and Albania under Tito's control and the outbreak of civil war in Greece seemingly going well for the Communists, the way seemed to be open for the realisation of the Balkan Federation project, which had been abandoned by the Comintern on the eve of the Second World War.

The 1948 watershed

The spectacular expulsion of the Yugoslav Party from the Cominform in June 1948 changed the situation completely. It demonstrated to the whole world that, far from enjoying Moscow's support for the setting up of a Balkan Federation, Tito had in this regard been acting against its wishes. The Soviet authorities had warned Tito to behave circumspectly so as not to embarrass it in its relations with the Western Allies, but he had ignored those warnings. It also became clear that, in Stalin's assessment, the charismatic Tito could not only cause Moscow trouble in its relations with the West, but also threaten its own hegemony in the new sphere of control it was in the process of establishing in the eastern and southern parts of Europe. The brief period of general puzzlement and uncertainty ended relatively quickly and the Great Power 50:50 power ratio began to be re-established, at least as far as Yugoslavia was concerned. The Western Powers stepped in and started providing Yugoslavia with the financial, economic and military aid that Moscow had stopped giving it. Tito repaid the Western Powers by helping them out in Greece where the non-Communist government had for several years been engaged in a civil war against the Communist guerrilla movement. Tito, who had been the principal backer of the Communist side in Greece, ordered in July 1949 the closure of the Greek-Yugoslav border and, at the same time, ended military and economic support for the Communist guerrillas, thus helping Greece's pro-Western government to victory.

This behaviour and other subsequent examples of Yugoslavia's independence from the Soviet Union (notably its refusal to agree to repeated Soviet demands for naval and air bases on its territory) were appreciated by Western governments. They also hoped that Tito's example might help gradually undermine Soviet control of Eastern Europe. For the next three decades Tito's Yugoslavia continued to enjoy Western economic, political and, for a time, direct military support. However, early Western hopes that 'Titoism' might turn into an instrument for rupturing the entire Soviet bloc in Eastern Europe did not materialise. This was not least due to Moscow's determination to maintain its control at any cost, as demonstrated by a series of harsh purges of alleged 'Titoists' after 1948 in Albania, Bulgaria, Hungary, Czechoslovakia and Poland. Later this determination to hang on to Eastern Europe was demonstrated, first, by the use of armed force in 1956 to stop Hungary adopting the multi–party system and, in foreign affairs, neutrality between East and West and, second, in 1968 in Czechoslovakia to stop it from moving towards multi–party democracy and economic pluralism.

An important feature of the East-West standoff in Yugoslavia was the fact that Tito, though in foreign affairs not committed to either side in the Cold War, retained at home a variant of the Communist system. This represented, in Moscow's eyes, an important guarantee. After a thaw in Soviet-Yugoslav relations, which followed Stalin's death in 1953, there was a steady development of relations between Moscow and Belgrade. And so, despite occasional political and ideological tiffs with Belgrade, Moscow supplied it with arms and raw materials and offered an important market for Yugoslav exports. East-West competition for Yugoslavia suited Tito admirably. In the mid-1950s, he increased his freedom of manoeuvre by becoming one of the leaders of the non-aligned movement, consisting chiefly of countries that had been under Western colonial rule. The standoff over Yugoslavia between the Soviet Union and the West remained in force for more than three decades and lasted for a while even after Tito's death in 1980.

The road to change: Albania, Bulgaria and Romania

The first half of the 1990s was a time of high drama in post-Tito Yugoslavia, involving the violent break-up of the country with the accompanying mayhem and destruction of life and property. It also resulted eventually in the setting up of six successor states (Bosnia and Herzegovina, Croatia, Macedonia, Montenegro, Serbia and Slovenia) as well as, in 2008, a formal declaration of independence by Kosovo, which was recognised by many countries. These events are discussed later in this chapter and in the next one. In contrast, the other Balkan states—Albania, Bulgaria and Romania—managed to avoid the calamitous circumstances that befell their neighbour. But they, too, went through periods of extreme upheaval.

Albania

At the end of the Second World War, Albania signed an agreement under which the Soviet Union would supply grain and technical assistance for the oil and mineral extraction industries in return for Albanian tobacco, fruit preserves, copper ore and oil. For Albania, close relations with Moscow of necessity also meant close relations with the Tito regime in Belgrade, which Albania's Communist leader, Enver Hoxha had strong misgivings about. He feared, with good reason, that Albania might end up by being not only dominated by its bigger Communist neighbour, Yugoslavia, but actually swallowed up by it. By 1948 Yugoslavia was ready to implement the plan (noted earlier) for a union with Albania, but then came the Tito-Stalin quarrel. Hoxha backed Stalin and at the same time got rid of his pro-Yugoslav rival, Xoxe.

Albania did well out of the Soviet-Yugoslav dispute, obtaining from its patron, the Soviet Union significant financial help for various projects as well as a military security guarantee against the West, which had been trying to undermine the Albanian regime. However, there was friction over the Soviet decision to stop investing in the development of the Albanian oil industry. There was another, more important cause of friction. In the mid-1950s, under Nikita Khruschev's leadership, the Soviet Union improved its relations with Yugoslavia and wanted Albania to follow suit. Hoxha, who in any case disapproved of the Soviet leader's de-Stalinisation policy, refused. In 1960 it began to look as if Albania might be abandoned by the Soviet Union as part of a developing Soviet-Yugoslav rapprochement. The open breach came in the second half of 1960 and ushered in an extremely difficult period for Albania. In the course of 1961, Soviet submarines were withdrawn from the naval base at Vlorë, Soviet and East European credits were cancelled, advisers were withdrawn, and Albanian students were expelled from Soviet and East European universities. Albanian ships being repaired in Soviet yards were seized and diplomatic relations with Albania were broken off. However, the outbreak of the Sino-Soviet dispute presented the Albanians with a lifeline in the shape of a new, if distant, patron in Peking (now Beijing).

China promptly stepped in and announced that it was giving Albania roughly what the Soviet bloc would have offered. Aid worth US$132 million was provided and 6,000 Chinese specialists were sent to replace those from the Soviet bloc on projects such as the construction of the new steel complex in Elbasan. Under Chinese influence, Albanian agriculture was fully collectivised. Private animal rearing was banned and all livestock had to be brought into the collective farms. Peasant markets were banned to eliminate private trading in foodstuffs produced on the private plots, which were reduced in size. A striking manifestation of Chinese influence was the abolition of religion in 1967 when Hoxha proclaimed Albania as the first atheist state in the world. The alliance with China provided an important boost to the Albanian regime. China also benefited from the arrangement. It was from powerful, Chinese-built radio transmitters in Albania that Peking broadcast its political and ideological message to the Soviet bloc as well as to the non-Communist part of Europe. Small Albania became, with China, the Mecca of 'pure' Marxist-Leninists from all over the world.

It came as a shock to Albania when China established diplomatic and commercial relations with the United States, following a visit by President Richard Nixon in 1972, and also re-established relations with Yugoslavia. The Albanians were encouraged by China to do the same and stop relying exclusively on Chinese aid and even to seek aid from the West. In 1978, China suspended its aid to Albania. Chinese advisers were recalled and Albanian students in China were sent home. However, Albania was helped by the fact that by the mid-1970s it had become self-sufficient in grain, oil and electricity. After Enver Hoxha's death in 1985, his successor Ramiz Alia tried to take the country out of its isolation. Relations with Greece improved when in 1987 Athens decided to end the formal state of war that still existed with Albania. However, the Kosovo issue was one of a number of obstacles to improved relations with Yugoslavia. New contacts were sought in Europe beyond the Balkans. Albania managed to find new commercial partners (though no new political patron) in the West. Economic relations with West Germany were stimulated by the establishment of diplomatic relations in 1987, following visits to Albania by Franz-Josef Strauss, a senior German political figure and former Defence Minister.

In internal affairs, Alia maintained his predecessor's firm line, but the regime could not withstand the impact of dramatic changes in Central Europe. In December 1989 and January 1990 there were anti–government protests in Shkodra in the north. Before that, some political prisoners had been included in a general amnesty, but the gesture had whetted rather than satisfied the appetite for change and reform. In April 1990 Alia announced that relations would be restored with both the Soviet Union and the United States. In May, the National Assembly adopted a law allowing foreign investment in Albania. The penal code was relaxed and the right to practise religion was restored. In December 1990 the legalisation of political parties was permitted. In April 1991 the Marxist-inspired constitution was abandoned and replaced by an interim one, guaranteeing multi–party democracy and economic liberalisation. All those changes took place against the background of mounting political and social unrest.

The elections, held on 31 March and 7 and 14 April 1991, were won by the Communists, who took 60 per cent of the vote and 169 of the 250 seats in the National Assembly. There were charges of electoral fraud, but the Communists managed to hold on to the rural vote, while the towns went to the opposition. Alia failed to hang on to his seat in Tirana. He remained President, but there were two changes of Prime

Minister within a year. Fatos Nano was appointed after serious disturbances in February but, following further disturbances in May, a 'government of national stability' was formed in June under Ylli Bufi that included opposition representatives. In December that year, following further disorders, a non-party figure, Vilson Ahmeti was appointed. It was obvious that parts of the country were out of the government's control and that the Communists were losing the grip on power, but there were huge problems facing the country.

Those problems were made particularly difficult by Albania's lack of democratic tradition and by its extreme poverty, the latter being the legacy of its ultra-isolationist brand of Communism. The economic misery—made more intolerable by many Albanians' ability over the years to watch Italian, Greek and Yugoslav television—sparked off the revolts in 1990–91 and led to the attempted mass exodus to Greece, Yugoslavia and, across the Adriatic, to Italy. Ultimately, this led to the collapse of the Communist regime. In an attempt to calm the situation, the next parliamentary elections were brought forward to March 1992. The elections were held under a new electoral system, with 100 members of parliament being elected in single-member constituencies on the basis of winning a relative majority, and a further forty elected on the basis of proportional representation and with a 4 per cent threshold for securing seats in parliament.

The elections produced a massive victory for the opposition Democratic Party of Albania (PDS), which won ninety-two seats to thirty-eight for the Communists. Its leader, Sali Berisha was elected President. Aleksander Meksi, an engineer, was appointed Prime Minister. The Communists were at long last routed, and the government made a promising reforming start, which included the rapid dismantling of the country's collectivised agricultural system and a degree of privatisation of public-sector enterprises. However, food shortages and soaring prices continued to fuel unrest. By the second half of 1992, Albania started receiving food aid as well as financial loans from Western states and international financial institutions. Gradually, a degree of social stability was achieved.

After years of international isolation Albania started being integrated into the world community, cultivating particularly close relations with the United States In February 1994, it joined NATO's Partnership for Peace Programme under which American troops took part in manoeuvres in Albania in March and July of that year. The Americans were allowed to use Albanian territory for launching unmanned reconnaissance aircraft over Bosnia and Herzegovina as part of NATO's operations there. Relations with Greece deteriorated in 1993 over Albanian complaints that Greece was trying to 'Hellenise' the Albanians in the south of the country and using the Greek Orthodox Church in the process. Following the arrest of a Greek Orthodox priest, Greece expelled thousands of illegal Albanian immigrants back to Albania and blocked a credit the European Union had authorised for Albania to help ease its trade deficit. Tensions rose further in 1994 when the Albanian authorities arrested five ethnic Greeks following a raid on an arms store in which two Albanian soldiers were killed. Greece sealed its border with Albania and expelled a further 70,000 illegal Albanian immigrants. By 1996 relations had improved sufficiently for a treaty of friendship to be signed with Greece in March of that year.

Bulgaria

Unlike in Albania, Greece and Yugoslavia where the local Communists were working with the grain of national feeling and were thus able to mobilise considerable public support in their bid for power during and after the Second World War, in Bulgaria the Communist Party really had to struggle. During the Second World War the situation in Bulgaria offered relatively little scope for revolutionary activity because the country had not been occupied and had made territorial gains from the war. King Boris III had for a while succeeded in keeping at bay the ever more powerful and aggressive Germany, which had been expanding its influence in Eastern and South-Eastern Europe, strengthened by its signing in August

17

1939 of the security and division-of-spheres pact with the Soviet Union. But in the end, he gave in and so, in March 1941, Bulgaria joined the Tripartite Pact (Germany, Italy and Japan), and allowed the entry of German troops. When the Germans and the Italians attacked and occupied Greece and Yugoslavia in April and partitioned the Balkans, Bulgaria's share was western Thrace and Serbian-ruled Macedonia minus a strip in the west under Italian rule.

Mindful of traditional pro-Russian feeling among the population, King Boris kept Bulgaria neutral when Germany attacked the Soviet Union in June 1941. Bulgaria faced a dilemma. If it broke with Germany, it would suffer a harsh German occupation—as the example of Hungary in March 1944 showed—but if it did not break with Germany in time, it would suffer subsequent Soviet occupation. Eventually, Bulgaria declared war on Germany on 8 September, but by then the Soviet troops had crossed into Bulgaria following a Soviet declaration of the war. Having changed sides under a new government formed on 9 September by the Fatherland Front, a coalition of left-of-centre parties as well as the Communists, Bulgaria was allowed to send its troops to fight on the Soviet side in Hungary and Austria where they suffered significant casualties. The Communists dominated the government from the start, but the Soviet-style one-party system took a long time to impose and was fully in place only at the end of 1947.

In its march to power, the Bulgarian Communist Party, operating at that time under the name of the Bulgarian Workers' Party, was helped by three factors. First, the non-Communists believed that the closeness of Communists to Moscow (notably that of people like Georgi Dimitrov, head of the Communist International in Moscow) could help prevent the imposition on Bulgaria of heavy war reparations. Bulgaria's economy had been badly hit by such reparations after the First World War, which it had also ended on the losing side. That feeling was so strong that the opposition held back for patriotic reasons. Second, the Communists were able to play on the Bulgarians' psychological need, understandable in a nation that had been repeatedly defeated in recent wars, for a powerful protector against a hostile world. Third, the Communists benefited from the absence from the country of the Bulgarian Army, fighting the Germans in Hungary and Austria, during the crucial period from the autumn of 1944 till the late spring of 1945.

However, none of this resulted in milder, more tolerant policies towards Bulgaria by the victors. The Allied refusal, taken with strong Soviet support, to grant Bulgaria co-belligerent status, despite its military participation on the Allied side in the autumn of 1944 and spring of 1945, meant the loss of all territories occupied by Bulgaria during the Second World War, except southern Dobrudja. Despite the fact that Bulgaria had not been occupied by a foreign power during the Second World War and had not been engaged in a war against the Soviet Union, more Bulgarians were accused of collaboration and war crimes than in any other East European country. Most prominent members of the opposition were 'liquidated' within six months of the Soviet Army's entry into Bulgaria. With Western governments showing little interest in Bulgaria, the Soviet Union, as head of the powerful Allied Control Commission (ACC), was able to shape events more or less at will.

The Communists' takeover was carried out in several stages. Their first target was the army, which was subjected to several purges to rid it of 'unreliable' elements. The Communists also took control of the radio and the distribution of newsprint. Their control of the Ministry of the Interior enabled them to establish a new police force subservient to them. Their control of the Ministry of Justice and, thus, the courts, similarly allowed the holding of a number of show trials of the remaining political opponents. The most spectacular of those was that of the leading non-Communist politician, Nikola Petkov, who was sentenced to death on trumped-up charges and hanged in August 1947. A referendum on the monarchy in September 1946 resulted in the declaration of a republic. The late King Boris's ten-year-old son, Simeon, was sent into exile. In February 1947 the peace treaty was signed, which led to the subsequent withdrawal of the Soviet Army. In December 1947 the Bulgarian parliament adopted the so-called Dimitrov Constitution, which declared Bulgaria a 'people's republic' and enshrined in law the state's total control of the economy, which had already been implemented in practice through systematic expropriations and confiscations of private property.

In the field of foreign policy, Yugoslavia's expulsion from the Cominform in June 1948 led to the reversal of a policy that had been agreed by Tito and Georgi Dimitrov, who had returned form Moscow in November 1945 and assumed a dominant role in Bulgaria. That policy, aimed at the formation of a Balkan Federation, included the provision that parts of Pirin Macedonia within Bulgaria should be ceded to Yugoslav Macedonia once the Balkan Federation had been established. In that region of Bulgaria the local population was being taught by teachers, brought from Yugoslav Macedonia, the Macedonian language that had been adopted as the official language there. In Bulgaria this was an immensely unpopular policy, which was quickly dropped after the break with Yugoslavia. That break was an excuse for a thorough purge of the Bulgarian Communist Party (BKP), as it started calling itself again in December 1948. In December 1949, Traicho Kostov, a popular figure in the Party was put on trial and sentenced to death. He was accused of pro-Titoist sympathies, but the real reason was that he had dared criticise Soviet economic policies. Some 100,000 Party members were expelled, and many of them were sent to labour camps. The excuse was the danger of 'national communism' as practised by Tito in Yugoslavia. Dimitrov himself died in Moscow from his various illnesses in July 1949.

Thus, stage-by-stage, Bulgaria was brought to heel and eventually acquired within the Soviet bloc the status of a docile satellite. Under Dimitrov's successor as Party leader and Prime Minister, Vulko Chervenkov, Bulgaria was thoroughly 'sovietised'. The Soviet model was applied to all sectors of national life, including the economy, the armed forces, education and culture, with Soviet advisers attached to all government departments. However, in contrast to Soviet practice, the Chervenkov regime allowed the emigration of almost all of Bulgaria's surviving Jews. As a concession to Bulgarian nationalism, some 162,000 Turks were 'encouraged' to emigrate from Dobrudja, the rich arable area being prepared for collectivisation.

There were material compensations for Bulgaria's Soviet orientation. Thanks partly to Soviet subsidies, Bulgaria's economy managed high annual growth rates during most of the 1970s. However, by the end of the decade it found itself in the midst of a serious economic crisis. Timid but hastily and ineptly implemented reforms, introduced by the regime of Todor Zhivkov in the early 1980s, produced serious disarray both in the economy and in the state administration. In late 1984 the regime decided to resort to nationalism once again by launching a campaign for the forcible 're-Bulgarianisation' of the country's Turkish minority, which accounted for about 10 per cent of the total population. Most of the minority's members were not, it was officially claimed, Turks but, rather, Bulgarians, who had been forcibly converted to Islam under Ottoman rule and had thus lost their Bulgarian national consciousness. A parallel campaign to encourage mass emigration of the Turkish minority to Turkey was also launched. In the summer of 1989 300,000 ethnic Turks left Bulgaria for Turkey. Many of them later returned, but this policy damaged Bulgaria's reputation abroad, while at home public support for the Zhivkov regime continued to decline.

Zhivkov was deposed in a palace coup in November 1989. In December, a number of non-communist political associations formed the Union of Democratic Forces (SDS). The SDS included environmentalist groups angry over large-scale damage to the natural environment caused by reckless government policies pursued both in industry and agriculture. The first post-Zhivkov government of Petur Mladenov allowed the formation of non-Communist political parties, released political prisoners and curbed the powers of the police. At the first multi–party elections in June 1990, the Bulgarian Socialist Party (BSP—the renamed Communist Party) won a majority, but found it hard to run the country. A new constitution was adopted in July 1991. Following the elections in October 1991 a non-Communist coalition government was formed by the SDS, with the support of the Movement for Rights and Freedom (DPS), a mainly ethnic Turkish party holding the balance in parliament.

The SDS-led coalition government started off with what seemed a good chance of pushing through the reformist policies upon which its leader, Filip Dimitrov, had campaigned. It pursued a sensible and constructive foreign policy. Relations with Turkey improved. On 16 January 1992 Bulgaria became the first country to recognise the newly independent Macedonian state. That step was welcomed by the governments of Western Europe and of the United States as an important contribution to the region's stability. However, it upset Greece, which had until then been a supporter of Bulgaria's attempt to establish closer relations with the European Community. Neither the Dimitrov government nor its successor, a cabinet made up of non-party experts formed in 1992 by Liuben Berov, managed to realise its potential. The return of property sequestrated under the Communist regime and the privatisation of land were achieved, but the original anti–Communist alliance rapidly fell apart against the background of a slowing reforming momentum and declining living standards.

Romania

Romania initially entered the Second World War against the Soviet Union on the German side in June 1941 and was rewarded by the return of the territories it had been forced to cede to the Soviet Union in 1940. It also gained Transnistria, a region between the Dniester and the Bug. However, Romania suffered heavy losses on the eastern front. The young

King Michael, who had in 1940 succeeded his father Carol after the latter had been forced into exile, managed to overthrow the pro-German leader, General Ion Antonescu. Romanian forces subsequently fought alongside the Soviet Army in Central Europe, but Romania still ended the war being treated as an enemy country.

There were two factors that helped Romanian Communists to gain and consolidate their power in 1944 and 1945. First, because the country had not experienced either civil war or physical devastation as a result of wartime operations on its territory, the state apparatus was intact and in place and, after purges in the army and the civil service, ready to serve the new regime. Second, the non-Communists still feared in the immediate post-armistice period that, since Romania was a former enemy country, the Western Allies might prevent it from regaining northern Transylvania, which had been awarded by the Axis Powers to Hungary in 1940. Soviet support was, therefore, seen as essential in securing this vital national objective and the Communists, as Moscow's friends, were seen as best placed to secure it. This tactic proved correct. Romania managed, with Stalin's backing, to get Transylvania back. This was a strong boost for the Communists.

The Communist power bid accelerated in May 1945. With the end of the war in Europe, the time was ripe for the liquidation of the non-Communist forces grouped round the King. One of the means of achieving this was the fostering of divisions among the other parties. The other was exploitation of political and other trials. The trial of Antonescu in 1946 helped in this respect by providing an opportunity of smearing the opposition figures like the most prominent democratic leader, Iulius Maniu, by (falsely) linking them to Antonescu and his regime. Then there was electoral cheating on a large scale in the November 1946 elections, as well as terror and intimidation. The non-Communist parties were destroyed by the end of 1947. Many political leaders and activists, including Maniu, were imprisoned after being tried for allegedly collaborating with British and US secret services. Maniu died

23

in prison in 1953. The King was forced to abdicate on 30 November 1947 and left Romania early in January 1948. In April 1948 the National Assembly, elected a month earlier, passed a new Constitution based on that of the Soviet Union, which declared Romania a People's Democracy. In the summer of 1948 the Assembly passed a law nationalising industrial, banking, insurance, mining and transport companies.

Unlike Bulgaria, Romania had oil and was rich in raw materials. It was, in the immediate post-1945 period, the eastern European country most exploited by the Soviet Union. Merchant ships and railway rolling stock were impounded and transported to the Soviet Union, as were large quantities of industrial and semi–manufactured goods. The Soviet-Romanian joint-stock companies controlled all sectors of economic life. Romanian exports to, and imports from, the Soviet Union were subject to price discrimination. Even later on, in the second half of the 1950s and the early 1960s, when the Soviet Union started to shore up the troubled East European economies, Romania remained bottom of the list—despite the fact that it was a key supplier to the Soviet economy of oil products, uranium, timber and foodstuffs. The gap between Romania and the more advanced East European countries widened, with the prospect—at the time perceived as intolerable by the Communists and non-Communists alike—that Romania would remain the lowly supplier of food and raw materials to the industrialised parts of the Soviet bloc. The tight Soviet grip on the Romanian economy reinforced the already strong anti–Soviet feeling among the population. Most important, the knowledge that Romania was being discriminated against in comparison with the other East European countries caused intense frustration to many in the Romanian ruling group.

Stalin's death in March 1953 left Romania's hard-line and deeply unpopular leadership in an exposed position. Its sense of vulnerability increased with the onset of the de-Stalinisation campaign in February 1956 and culminated in the autumn of 1956 with the political upheaval in Poland and the outbreak of the Hungarian revolution, with its political echoes among the large Hungarian minority in Transylavania. The withdrawal in 1958 of Soviet troops, stationed in the country since 1944, provoked a search for a replacement of the political guarantee to the regime they had represented. The Sino-Soviet split which occurred shortly thereafter created a new situation, offering the deeply unpopular Romanian regime a chance to play the nationalist card.

The ruling group united behind the party leader, Gheorge Gheorghiu-Dej, a 'home Communist' who had spent the 1933–44 period in Romanian prisons. The cause of Romania's modernisation and industrialisation appealed to the party elite and the ordinary people. Gheorghiu-Dej and his colleagues, notably Nicolae Ceauşescu, who succeeded him on his death in 1965, simply broadened this into a direct appeal to Romanian nationalism in every other sphere. They were playing upon the feelings which some of them had in any case shared with their non-Communist fellow-Romanians—above all a view of Romania as a superior island of Latinity surrounded by a Slav sea. That was why the regime's new, openly nationalist policy had a strong cultural content. However, though the stress in the 1960s and the 1970s was on an anti–Russian platform, it was kept within very careful limits. This was to avoid challenging Moscow on any important issue—not least over Bessarabia, which had become the Moldavian Soviet Republic after 1945. Ceauşescu's defiance of Moscow was never considered a serious threat to the Soviet Union. Surrounded by Communist states, Romania was in no position to switch alliances. The regime was, as Moscow knew very well, never going to establish multi–party democracy and, in fact, relied on its Soviet connection as the ultimate guarantee of its domestic power.

Meanwhile, a variety of high-profile international issues brought the regime substantial gains, in the shape of prestigious visits to Washington, London and other Western capitals. In 1969 President Nixon visited Romania, the first American President to visit the Communist-ruled part of Europe. There were also other, more tangible gains. Romania was granted the most-favoured-nation status by the United States and was admitted to the Generalised Agreement on Trade and Tariffs (GATT) in 1971 and to the IMF in 1972, the first East European state to be granted membership. However, serious mistakes and miscalculations in economic policy, especially over energy, led to a large increase in hard-currency debt, which Ceauşescu insisted on paying back in full. The price was heavy. Imports were drastically cut and everything that could be sold abroad, including foodstuffs, was exported. The resulting food and fuel shortages caused widespread resentment. There was also public anger over grandiose and expensive regime projects, such as the reconstruction of the Bucharest city centre, and, in the countryside, the destruction of old villages and the forcible transfer of their populations into 'agrotowns'. However, right up to November 1989 the Ceauşescu's regime seemed to be unaffected by the ferment elsewhere in the Communist-ruled part of Europe. But on 21 and 22 December 1989, Ceauşescu, just back from a visit to Iran, was heckled while speaking at public meetings in Bucharest and was eventually forced to flee. The army sided with a new body called the National Salvation Front (FSN). Some elements in the security forces continued to resist for a few days, but their resistance stopped on 27 December, two days after Ceauşescu and his wife were captured and shot.

Despite the fact that the FSN had stage-managed the fall of Ceauşescu and that power stayed in the hands of the Communists, the new regime was interested in change. An FSN government, drawn from the reformist forces within the Communist Party, was formed under Petre Roman as Prime Minister. Ion Iliescu, a former close but later discarded associate of Ceauşescu, became President. The FSN said it was committed to managing the transition from one-party rule to democracy, but to doing so cautiously. No purges were carried out in the local government or the trade unions. The free-market system was rejected and the national control of the economy was to be maintained. But the new regime abandoned the notorious 1980s 'systematisation' programme, which had been designed to break up Hungarian communities in Transylavnia and drown their culture in the new, predominantly Romanian agro-complexes. There were improvements for the Hungarian minority in broadcasting and education. The remaining members of the other minority, the Germans, whom the regime had been allowing to emigrate in return for D-Marks from the then West German government, were allowed to emigrate freely and most of them left. The population welcomed the resumption of food imports, which had not been allowed under Ceauşescu's policy of forced exports to save the regime from indebtedness to the West—even if the population went short.

At the elections in May 1990, the FSN scored an easy victory, winning two-thirds of the seats in both houses of parliament. Iliescu won the presidential election and was re-elected in 1992. After the first multi–party election in Romania held in February 1992, there was a swing away from the FSN. The Democratic Convention of Romania (CDR) made considerable gains. In March 1992 the FSN was further weakened by the formation, under Petru Roman's leadership, of a dissident faction retaining the name FSN. But the majority faction, under the new name of the Democratic National Salvation Front (FDSN), and led by Iliescu, still emerged with a majority in the national elections held in September 1992, pushing the CDR into second and Roman's FSN into third place. In the presidential election Iliescu defeated Emil Constantinescu, Rector of Bucharest University, in the second round. Nicolae Văcăriou formed a government mostly made up of non-party experts and some members of the FDSN. Văcăriou remained Prime Minister until 1996, but increasingly came to rely on extreme nationalist and neo-Communist groups. In economic policy, the privatisation drive was slowed down. The government continued to subsidise the loss-making enterprises as well as giving large subsidies to agriculture. The government's attempts to bring Romania closer to NATO and the EU were slow to show results and the Romanian population was disappointed by the fact that Romania was lagging behind other post-Communist states in terms of international integration. Relations with Russia and Ukraine remained complicated by a number of outstanding territorial issues and other issues from the past.

Irretrievable breakdown in Yugoslavia

There had been no shortage of warning signals since the late 1980s about a coming political earthquake in Yugoslavia. In November 1990, a report by the CIA, leaked to The International Herald Tribune and published on 29 November 1990, warned that a war in Yugoslavia leading to the country's disintegration was likely within eighteen months (for the full de-classified text of the CIA paper, see 'Transformed National Intelligence Estimate NIE-90, October 1990', in 'Yugoslavia: From "National Communism" to National Collapse', US Intelligence Community Estimate Products on Yugoslavia, 1948–1990, pp. 653–674). Yet when the war in Yugoslavia broke out in June 1991, international opinion was surprised. It should not have been. Yugoslavia's slow-motion dissolution had been in progress for some considerable time.

Whether or not its ultimate demise was 'inevitable' is a meaningless, a-historical question, but that will of course not prevent it from being discussed for generations to come. We know that from the example of those endless, mostly totally futile and misplaced discussions about the inevitability or otherwise of the collapse of various multinational entities in modern times—from the Habsburg, Russian and Ottoman Empires at the end of the First World War to that of the British, Dutch, French and Portuguese Empires after the Second and that of the Soviet Union in our own time. That being said, what was truly surprising was that it took so many people—including the multitude of 'Yugoslavists' who had been studying the country for decades professionally—so long to grasp that the glue that had helped keep post-1945 Yugoslavia together had dissolved during the 1980s, and to consider the implications.

Tito, the charismatic leader, who had skilfully manipulated (and arbitrated among) all the different Yugoslav nationalities within a six–republic federation had died in May 1980, aged eighty-seven. His demise had been followed, a decade later, by that of the ruling League of Communists of Yugoslavia (as the Communist Party of Yugoslavia was renamed in 1952), which he had led since 1937. The LCY congress in Belgrade, held from 20 to 22 January 1990, rejected a request from the Slovene and Croat Communists that the LCY's leading role should be formally abolished and that the constituent parties in the six federal republics (Bosnia and Herzegovina, Croatia, Macedonia, Montenegro, Serbia and Slovenia) should form a union of independent parties. Thereupon, the delegates from Croatia and Slovenia left. The Congress adjourned and was never reconvened.

Yugoslavia's economic prosperity, based largely on massive Western external assistance in the 1950s and 1960s and, in the 1970s, on extensive external borrowing, which in the last two decades of Tito's rule had created a mood of optimism and hope, had ended. For a long time, Yugoslavia had been living beyond its means, amassing by 1981 a huge external debt. Hopes that the country might embark on radical free-market reforms had been raised by the appointment, with strong backing from Western states, of Ante Marković as Yugoslavia's Prime Minister in March 1989. Marković was a former industrial manager who had also served as Prime Minister and, later, also as President of the Croatian republic within the Yugoslav federation. In December 1989 Marković's government pegged the Yugoslav dinar to the Deutschmark (at the rate of 7:1) and made it freely convertible, having previously amassed more than US$10 billion worth of hard-currency reserves. Inflation was halted almost immediately. Other fundamental reforms launched by Marković were aimed at turning Yugoslavia into a free-market economy in all but name. They included a reform of enterprises, which effectively abolished the inefficient and expensive self-management system; and that of the banking system, which restored the independence of the banks from local political groups. But there was no political consensus among the Yugoslav republics in favour of the Marković programme. It remained stalled as result of opposition from various quarters, especially Serbia, Yugoslavia's largest republic. Serbia strongly objected to Marković's import liberalisation policy and his drastic squeeze on credit to loss-making enterprises, seeing both—quite correctly—as a threat to its bankrupt industries.

The sense of external danger from the Soviet Union, which had helped maintain a sort of national unity since Yugoslavia's expulsion from the Soviet bloc in 1948, had totally disappeared by the late 1980s. It was no longer the foreign enemy but the enemy (or enemies) within that seemed to preoccupy the peoples of Yugoslavia. Moreover, quite suddenly, it had become possible for those peoples to start looking for new external alignments and to do so without fear of opening the door to the Soviet Army and the KGB. Also, the prospect of Yugoslavia being offered associate membership of the European Community lessened the attraction of Titoist non-alignment policy

The developments in Yugoslavia were a serious cause of worry for its neighbours in the region. After the Second World War, in striking contrast to the period leading up to it, none of the neighbouring states harboured territorial designs on Yugoslavia. On the contrary, all were in favour of Yugoslavia's survival as a state. This attitude was emphatically shared by the Western Powers, whose chief interest was in the maintenance of stability in South-Eastern Europe. Therefore, any mayhem occurring in Yugoslavia was likely to come from within, from an internal implosion rather than from an explosion detonated from outside. That was exactly how it turned out; Yugoslavia became the epicentre of a powerful internal earthquake that continued to shake the whole region for over a decade

Long before Yugoslavia had begun to disintegrate, the speculation in the country as well as abroad centred on the role that the Yugoslav People's Army (JNA), sometimes referred to as Yugoslavia's 'seventh republic', might play in a crisis. The JNA leadership was indeed worried by the prospect of Yugoslavia evolving into a loose confederation, let alone splitting into several smaller states. As the sole remaining Titoist institution in the country since the *de facto* break-up of the LCY in January 1990, the JNA feared the loss both of its legitimacy and of its hitherto secure financial base. Besides, with 96 per cent of its officers LCY members, the JNA viewed the arrival to power in 1990 of non-Communist governments (elected in free, multi–party elections) in Croatia and Slovenia (and the coalition ones in Bosnia and Herzegovina and Macedonia), as a grave threat to the country's socialist system, of which it regarded itself as guarantor. But the army leadership was confused and divided over what to do. In the first half of 1991, JNA leaders were preparing for a state of emergency, but when they failed to get the support of the majority in the collective eight-member Presidency of Yugoslavia, the JNA's commander-in-chief, the project was abandoned. However, that failure had the effect of gradually bringing the Titoist JNA leadership, anxious to preserve Yugoslavia, steadily closer to the emerging new Serbian political establishment. This was made easier by the fact that the majority of officers were ethnic Serbs. Made up of Communists and non-Communist nationalists, this group shared the JNA's fears about the future of Yugoslavia, but the focus of its concerns was different. The main item on its political agenda was rolling back Yugoslavia's federal system, as enshrined in the 1974 Constitution.

According to the majority of Serbs, Communists and non-Communist alike, behind that Constitution lay the deliberate intention to weaken Serbia, and it had succeeded in doing so. The Serb case against Tito's federal Yugoslavia was most forcefully set out, not in a Party document, but in a memorandum by a working group in the Serbian Academy of Sciences in Belgrade. Some of the Memorandum's critics in the other Yugoslav republics saw in it echoes of the famous

Načertanije, the 1844 national programme for a Greater Serbia as the successor to the short-lived 14th-century Serbian state of King Stefan Dušan. Other critics thought it reflected the nostalgia increasingly felt by many Serbs for the first royalist Yugoslavia (1918–1941), in which, despite its many shortcomings from the Serbian point of view, the Serbs played the role of the leading nation, which they never fully recovered in the post-1945 federal Yugoslavia rebuilt by Tito.

The main thesis of the Memorandum, leaked to the press in 1986 while still in draft form, was that the Serbs, Yugoslavia's largest nation with a 36 per cent share of the total population, had been politically discriminated and economically disadvantaged in the post-1945 federation under Tito, a Croat, and his Slovene deputy, Edvard Kardelj, The document called for the abolition of the 1974 Constitution as the embodiment of the principle 'strong Yugoslavia, weak Serbia' allegedly pursued under Tito. There were three specific objections to Titoist Yugoslavia from the Serbian point of view:

(1) The federal government's alleged discriminatory policy against Serbia in the economic field, reflected in the alleged predominance in economic decision-making ever since 1945, of Croatia and Slovenia, the two western republics;

(2) The allegedly deliberate splitting in 1974—so as to weaken the overall position of the Serbs in Yugoslavia—of the Serbian republic of the Yugoslav federation into three parts: Serbia proper, and the autonomous provinces of Kosovo and Vojvodina, with the two provinces directly participating in decision-making at the federal level and thus by-passing Serbia proper;

(3) The allegedly anti–Serb policy pursued in Kosovo by ethnic Albanian 'separatists' and 'irredentists', which the authors blamed for the steady exodus of the province's Serbs. The Memorandum also claimed that the Serbs in Croatia were being subjected to discrimination and a *de facto* assimilation.

If the Memorandum provided a conceptual basis for the Serb anti–federal backlash in Yugoslavia in the post-Tito period, it found its practical enforcer in Slobodan Milošević. Widely perceived (not least by foreign diplomats in Belgrade) as a moderate, able and modern-minded Party apparatchik, Milošević was routinely appointed as part of the established rotation procedure to the post of Communist Party leader in Serbia in 1986. A year later, in the autumn of 1987, he shocked both his Party sponsors and his Western admirers by taking full power and carrying out a widespread Party and government purge that eliminated, among others, his reformist mentor, Ivan Stambolić and a number of other reformminded officials. In 1988–89 Milošević broadened the Party's political base in Serbia by aligning himself quite openly with Serb nationalists, including those in the Serbian Academy of Sciences. The 'anti–bureaucratic revolution', as the Serb campaign of re-assertion was officially called, was ready to start.

The first target was Vojvodina. It was captured by pro-Milošević forces in the autumn of 1988, by a combination of political pressure and intimidation by supporters bussed in from other parts of Serbia. This most prosperous part of Serbia was until 1918 a part of Hungary. Until the end of the Second World War it had sizeable Hungarian and German minorities as well as Croats, Romanians and some others. Vojvodina had, since 1974, enjoyed the same status as Kosovo, namely, that of an autonomous province of Serbia, but with a seat on the eight-member collective presidency of Yugoslavia alongside the six 'full' republics. Like Kosovo, it had its own courts, police and territorial defence and was run by an autonomy-minded and relatively liberal leadership. Vojvodina's leaders proved relatively easy to topple, not least because the province had an ethnic Serbian majority, augmented since 1945 by steady ethnic Serbian immigration from other parts of Yugoslavia. This was matched, following the flight of some of the Germans in 1944 and the expulsion of the rest after 1945–46, by a steady emigration of the non-Serbs. The new Serbian immigrants, called *dođoši* (literally, the arrived ones), proved easier to radicalise than the old-settled Serbs.

Next came Montenegro. Pro-Milošević forces in a popular coup established political control in January 1989. For centuries, the poor mountain principality had been independent and it became a kingdom in 1910. It expanded its territory in the Balkan wars against the Ottoman Empire in 1912–1913. Having sided with Serbia against Austria-Hungary in 1914, it ended up by being occupied from 1915 to 1918. A controversial referendum held following the retreat of the occupying forces overthrew the Montenegrin dynasty and decided in favour of Montenenegro's union with Serbia. Opponents of the union with Serbia claimed that the referendum had been manipulated. Montenegro was occupied by Italy from 1941 to 1943. Strongly represented on the Tito Partisan side during the Second World War, Montenegro was in 1945 established as a republic within the Yugoslav federation. This represented a victory for those who argued that, for all their close historic ties with the Serbs, the Montenegrins had always been a separate people. That had been the view of the opponents of the union with Serbia in 1918, popularly known as the Greens (from the green-coloured ballot-slip used in the referendum). The four-and-a-half decades of predominance of revived pro-Green ideas in Montenegro's cultural and political life ended in January 1989 with the victory of an updated version of the old 'unitarists', who had campaigned—echoing Milošević—under the slogan that Serbia and Montenegro were but 'two eyes in one [Serbian] head'. Gaining political control over Montenegro was important to Milošević, because it secured for him Montenegro's vote in Yugoslavia's collective presidency.

In Bosnia and Herzegovina, Milošević's local associates, led by Radovan Karadžić, a native Montenegrin, had begun in 1987 to organise the local Serbs (32 per cent of the republic's total population, according to the 1981 census) in opposition to the tripartite government in Sarajevo. Bosnia's Serbs were told that they faced the danger of being 'swamped' by the fast-reproducing Moslems (39.5 per cent of the total) and that, since Bosnia was heading for a 'fundamentalist' Moslem-dominated government, the local Serbs needed arms to protect themselves. Arms and ammunition were provided secretly for pro-Milošević groups by the JNA.

In Croatia a similar scare campaign by Serbian newspapers and magazines and by Belgrade TV and actively aided by the Serbian Orthodox Church, was launched among the republic's sizeable Serb minority (12 per cent of the population). Local Serbs were bombarded with material aimed at reviving memories of the genocide, perpetrated under the German and Italian occupation, against Croatian Serbs by the quisling Ustaša regime of Ante Pavelić in 1941–1942. The aim was to convince the Croatian Serbs that they were once again confronted by the spectre of genocide. The secret arming of the pro-Milošević elements among the Croatian Serbs had begun in 1987–88. The media campaign, directed from Belgrade and highlighting the alleged threat of another genocide against the Serbs, helped radicalise Serbian opinion throughout Yugoslavia in support of Milošević's drive to secure as much of Yugoslavia as could be seized by playing the Serbian ethnic card. (That was not possible in Slovenia and Macedonia, where the number of ethnic Serbs was negligible.)

Kosovo, an autonomous province with a large ethnic Albanian majority, had (like Vojvodina) since 1974 had its own courts, police and territorial defence as well as a vote in Yugoslavia's collective presidency. By the late 1980s, partly due to the local Albanians' high birth-rate and partly to continuing Serb emigration from Kosovo, the Serbs' share in the province's total population had dropped to below 10 per cent. This was a bitter blow to many Serbs, because Kosovo had since the nineteenth century been the centrepiece of the Serbian national myth built round the story of Serb defeat by the Ottoman army in Kosovo in 1389, followed by four centuries from 1455 to 1860 of life under Ottoman rule. It was only in 1912 that Serbia had recaptured Kosovo, following the ailing Ottoman Empire's defeat in a war waged on it by a coalition of four Balkan states: Bulgaria, Greece, Montenegro and Serbia.

In March and April 1981, less than a year after Tito's death, there were student demonstrations in Kosovo in favour of the province being given the status of a full federal republic (though within the Yugoslav federation). The demonstrations were suppressed by force, and they were seen by many in Serbia as confirming their fears that Kosovo might try to split off from Yugoslavia. By late 1985 the condition of Serbs in Kosovo had begun to preoccupy mainstream opinion in Serbia and by 1987 the province had become the cornerstone of Serbian nationalism, with 60,000 Kosovo Serbs signing a petition against genocide allegedly practised there against their kind. In April 1987 Milošević visited Kosovo and promised the local Serbs 'No one should dare to beat you again!'. On 28 March 1989 Serbia's Assembly adopted constitutional amendments that gave the Serbian authorities in Belgrade direct control over Kosovo's police, courts and territorial defence, with an extra amendment enabling Serbia's Assembly to take decisions affecting Kosovo without first consulting that province's own assembly.

New laws, passed that same year, made it a crime for ethnic Albanians to buy or sell property without special permission of the authorities. Thousands of ethnic Albanians were dismissed from their jobs as doctors, teachers, police officers and key employees in state-owned firms and replaced with Serbs. Kosovo Albanian teachers and lecturers set up an Albanian-language education system in private houses, cellars, garages and wherever else they could. Parallel structures were established in health, education and other areas, funded by the Albanian diaspora in the West. Meanwhile, arbitrary arrest and police violence directed towards the Albanians became routine practice, earning Kosovo the reputation as the region with some of the worst human rights violations in all of Europe.

In October 1991 Kosovo's ethnic Albanian leaders, including many members of the by then forcibly dissolved provincial assembly, met secretly and declared Kosovo (in Albanian, *Kosova*) a 'sovereign and independent state'. In December 1991, when the European Community offered to extend recognition to the Yugoslav republics seeking independence, Kosovo's request for recognition was ignored. In 1992 Ibrahim Rugova, leader of the Democratic League of Kosovo (LDK) was elected president at semi–underground elections, tolerated but not regarded as valid by the Belgrade authorities. Milošević's re-annexation of Kosovo raised his popularity to unprecedented heights with the Serbs—not just those in Serbia proper and in Kosovo and Vojvodina, but also those in Bosnia and Herzegovina and Croatia. His success in presenting himself as the champion of all Serbs throughout Yugoslavia was an important factor in the electoral victory of his Socialist (the renamed Communist) Party of Serbia (SPS) in December 1990 and his re-election as President of Serbia with a large majority. The fact that ethnic Albanians in Kosovo had boycotted the elections *en masse* gave his SPS extra uncontested seats in the Serbian Assembly in Belgrade.

The Milošević-led campaign of Serb reassertion alarmed Yugoslavia's non-Serb majority. By 1989 Milošević's Serbia had gained three extra seats—those of Kosovo, Montenegro and Vojvodina—to add to its own on the post-Tito eight-member collective state presidency of Yugoslavia, which had, since Tito's death, assumed the role of the JNA's commander-in-chief. Crucially, the presidency was the only body with the constitutional right to proclaim a state of emergency. Replying to critics in the other republics, Serbia's leaders, including Milošević, had been protesting all along that all they wanted was a 'functioning federation', which Yugoslavia certainly was not. However, to the country's non-Serbs it looked as if re-centralisation of Yugoslavia was what Serbia was after. It looked to them as if Serbia was acquiring both the constitutional instruments and the military muscle needed to re-impose the sort of dominance it had had in all spheres of public life in the old, royalist Yugoslavia. Kosovo's re-annexation by Serbia caused a lot of unease, especially in Croatia and Slovenia. Apart from political anxieties, there were also the related economic grievances. For example, Slovenia and Croatia resented the fact that Serbia alone dictated and executed official Yugoslav policy towards Kosovo while they, as the better-off republics, had to bear much of the large financial and manpower burdens of the ever more repressive police and military operations in Kosovo.

The sense of economic grievance was particularly strong in Slovenia, which had only 8 per cent of the total population of Yugoslavia but in the 1980s accounted for a third of Yugoslavia's GNP as well as a quarter of its total exports. Slovenia had demanded—and failed to get—a reduction in the large (and constantly rising) federal budget, in which the biggest items was expenditure on the JNA and on Yugoslavia's large civil service. Slovenia had repeatedly protested against the growing, often politically motivated Serbian anti–reform obstruction on the economic front from the mid-1980s onwards, including trade boycotts against Slovenia and special tariffs on Slovene goods to punish the republic for allowing its media, the freest in the then Yugoslavia, to publish critical items on Kosovo. To crown it all, there was, in December 1990, the Serbian National Bank's decision secretly to issue 18.3 billion dinars (US\$ 1.4 billion) of new money, without the permission of the National Bank of Yugoslavia, in order to make a loan to the Serbian government. The Serbian monetary raid enabled the Milošević regime to fund the large wage increases prior to the elections that month that helped give Milošević's Communists—under their new Socialist name—a huge victory. The monetary raid fatally undermined Ante Marković's economic reform programme, which had been drawn up as a condition for the IMF's agreement to a nine-year rescheduling of Yugoslavia's huge debt.

Both in Slovenia and in Croatia there was a growing realisation that Milošević, having repeatedly broken one of the fundamental rules of federal Yugoslavia—that one federal unit did not interfere in the affairs of another—was unlikely to stop. The greatest concern of the two republics' leaders, shared by the majority of their population, was the looming threat of the imposition of a new, strongly Serbian-flavoured centralist regime in Belgrade presided over by Milošević that would aim to curtail and, eventually, abolish the two republics' autonomy. They came to the conclusion that the time may have come for them to cut loose from Yugoslavia and that, in the new, benign external environment in Europe, they could actually afford to do so. It was important that both republics were enjoying good bilateral relations with their two Western neighbours, Austria and Italy. Regular denunciations of 'separatist nationalism' and 'bourgeois liberalism', addressed from Belgrade to the two western republics by the JNA's main organ, *Narodna Armija* (People's Army) and the rest of the Belgrade media, only fed the growing pro-independence sentiment in Croatia and Slovenia.

The road to war

On 15 March 1991, Borisav Jović, chairman of the rotating eight-member presidency of Yugoslavia and one of Slobodan Milošević's closest allies, sparked off a constitutional and political crisis by resigning as chairman of the presidency in protest against the presidency's rejection by a majority of one vote of the JNA request for the proclamation of a state of emergency. A group of generals had originally favoured a Yugoslav version of General Jaruzelski's military coup in Poland in 1981, but realised that in a semi–confederate Yugoslavia it would not be easy to impose. That forced them to look for what they regarded as second-best solutions, all of them based on a state of emergency. However, when it came to the vote in the collective state presidency, only Serbia voted for the proposed state of emergency. Later in the month Jović, a pro-Milošević Serb, withdrew his resignation, but his unsuccessful manoeuvre, obviously stage-managed by his ally Milošević, had left a bad taste. The next crisis came on 15 May, when it was the turn of Croatia's representative, Stipe Mesić to be elected as the collective presidency's chairman. Serbia and Montenegro tried to prevent his election, claiming that he was an anti–Communist and extreme Croatian nationalist, but they eventually gave up after forty-five days under strong pressure from the EU and the United States. That enabled Mesić to take over on 1 July as Yugoslavia's next but, as it turned out, also its last head of state.

In April 1990, a centre-right alliance called Demos had won a majority in the elections for the Slovene parliament. In May 1990 the centre-right Croatian Democratic Union (HDZ) under the leadership of Franjo Tuđman, a former JNA general, had been victorious in the elections to the Croatian parliament. Tuđman became Croatia's president, while Milan Kučan, the pro-reform leader of the Slovene Communists, became president there. By the end of 1990, all six republics had conducted elections. Strongly supported by their public opinion, the governments of Croatia and Slovenia embarked on a course that—though for a while keeping a door ajar for an accommodation with Serbia—was eventually to lead to independence. However, consideration of joint Croat-Slovene proposals for a looser, confederal structure, preserving a broad Yugoslav framework but at the same time protecting the non-Serb republics from a Serb takeover, was twice blocked at the federal level by the Serb-led voting bloc. On 19 May 1991 a referendum in Croatia produced a 94 per cent majority in favour of leaving Yugoslavia. A referendum held in Slovenia in December 1990 had already produced a large majority in favour of full independence. On 25 June 1991 first the Croat parliament and then, a few hours later, the Slovene one declared independence.

The JNA went into action in Slovenia in the early hours of 27 June, declaring that it was acting to seal off Slovenia's borders with Austria and Italy, which had been taken over by the Slovene police. The JNA's action was taken in a political vacuum because Yugoslavia's collective presidency, which alone had the constitutional authority to issue such an order, was not functioning. The order for action in Slovenia was in fact issued by the federal government and executed by Defence

Minister Veljko Kadijević and Interior Minister Petar Gra-čanin. The intervention in Slovenia did not go well for the JNA. It was both militarily and politically ill-equipped, in contrast to the less well-armed but politically highly-motivated and well-organised Slovene territorial defence forces. Not only did the Slovenes fight much better than the JNA had expected, but the hostile international reaction to the JNA's intervention evidently surprised the generals and the politicians in Belgrade alike. The war lasted only ten days. After three weeks, the JNA withdrew from Slovenia, having gratefully accepted the European Community's (as the EU was known then) face-saving diplomacy (see Chapter IV). It had in the meantime suffered few casualties, but quite a few desertions.

The war in Croatia, which had already begun before the JNA had managed to withdraw the bulk of its troops and heavy equipment from Slovenia, turned out to be more bloody and prolonged, but also far more successful from the JNA's point of view. Serb paramilitaries, both those recruited from the ranks of the Serb minority in Croatia and those trained and armed in Serbia and brought over from there, were used to draw out the poorly-armed and under-equipped Croat National Guard, which had been set up after the proclamation of independence in June 1991. The JNA used the tactic of intervening, ostensibly to separate the warring sides but in fact to help the Serb paramilitaries consolidate their gains and protect them from Croat counter-attacks. The Croat forces lacked heavy artillery, military aircraft and helicopters as well as rifles and ammunition. In contrast, the JNA trained, fed and supplied the Serb irregulars and provided them with safe communication lines and active protection whenever they came under pressure from the Croatian forces

It was in the course of the war in Croatia in 1991 that the JNA gradually became a truly Serb force, having lost all its conscripts and most of the officers from Croatia and Slovenia as well as most of those from Macedonia and some from Bosnia and Herzegovina. In Serbia and Montenegro, there was growing resistance against the recruitment for war, with many desertions. The JNA filled the gaps by relying more and more on paramilitary groups such as the Serbian Volunteer Guards, the White Eagles and others. The shortage of manpower led to growing reliance on artillery and air attacks, which in turn increased the number of civilian casualties and the amount of material devastation. This was an important factor in the destruction of Vukovar in eastern Croatia in November 1991 by besieging JNA and Serb paramilitary forces. Dubrovnik on the Adriatic coast was also heavily shelled. By the time the UN-brokered cease-fire came into force in Croatia in January 1992, the combined JNA/irregular operations in Croatia had brought under rebel Serb control just under a third of the republic's territory under the name of *Republika Srpska Krajina* (RSK), which was made up of three territorial units: eastern Slavonia (Srijem and Baranja), western Slavonia, and a part of central Croatia lying between its borders with Slovenia in the west and Bosnia and Herzegovina in the east. All those became so-called United Nations Protected Areas (UNPAs) where international UNPROFOR units were stationed.

The next stage of the military conflict began in Bosnia and Herzegovina in April 1992. The republic was of key importance in the army's eyes in view of its central strategic position in the region. It was also the main source of troops and arms (under Tito, many Yugoslav arms factories were situated in Bosnia and Herzegovina because of its distance both from Yugoslavia's eastern and western borders). Military preparations for securing Bosnia and Herzegovina had already been well under way when the referendum on independence took place on 29 February and 1 March 1992. Of the 64 per cent registered voters who took part in the referendum, 93 per cent voted for independence, with the republic's Bosniak Moslems and Croats voting solidly in favour and most of the Serbs abstaining. On 6 April 1992 Bosnia and Herzegovina was recognised as a sovereign state by the European Community (Croatia and Slovenia had been recognised on 15 January). But most of the republic's Serbs, a third of its total population, had followed the urging of Radovan Karadžić to boycott the referendum. Karadžić claimed that the Bosnian Serbs faced the threat of fundamentalist Moslem rule over the whole republic under President Alija Izetbegović.

There was a good deal of preparation and coordination on the Serbian side for what followed. Artillery positions had been established around major Bosnian cities, including Sarajevo, in the winter of 1991–92. The JNA's units with artillery and heavy armour were transferred into Bosnia and Herzegovina early in 1992 from Croatia after the conclusion of the ceasefire there. Meanwhile, multi–ethnic Bosnian territorial forces under the government in Sarajevo were being disarmed by the JNA (as they had been in Croatia in the spring of 1991). Karadžić's SDS supporters were receiving arms both from Serbia and from local JNA commanders in Bosnia and Herzegovina. Serb military preparations were matched by political ones, which culminated in the proclamation of independence of the *Republika Srpska* (Serbian Republic) on 4 April 1992, two days before Bosnia's recognition by the EC. On 30 March, following a series of incidents staged in various Bosnian cities (including Sarajevo), the JNA had announced that it was ready to 'protect' the Serbs of Bosnia. A well-publicised massacre carried out by Serb paramilitaries in Bijeljina, a town in the predominantly Moslem eastern part of Bosnia close to the border of Serbia, and other similar actions in the same region led to a mass flight of Moslems. Fighting soon spread to other parts of Bosnia, with the JNA and Serb paramilitaries trying to secure important communication centres, arms factories and other key assets, though not with equal success everywhere.

On 14 April, Izetbegović declared that Bosnia and Herzegovina was the subject of external aggression coordinated from Belgrade with Serb SDS leaders in Bosnia and Herzegovina. On 27 April he called upon the JNA either to withdraw from Bosnia and Herzegovina altogether or to comply with the Bosnian government's request that all military forces stationed there should be integrated into the Bosnian Territorial Army. On 19 May the JNA command in Belgrade ordered the withdrawal from Bosnia and Herzegovina of its personnel who were Serb or Montenegrin citizens. Some 14,000 army personnel withdrew but about 80,000, with their heavy weapons and equipment, stayed, having been formally transferred to the defence forces of the new Bosnian Serb republic. They were placed under the command of General Ratko Mladić, who had been a senior JNA commander in Croatia during the 1991 war and had been subsequently transferred to Sarajevo. Mladić's troops quickly surrounded and besieged Sarajevo.

The Serb offensive in the summer and autumn of 1992 led to the capture of about 70 per cent of the Bosnian territory. However, it failed in the ethnically mainly Croat western Herzgovina where a Croat force, under the command of a body called the Croat Defence Council (HVO), supplied from Croatia and supported by Bosniak Moslem troops loyal to the Sarajevo government, managed to beat off the combined attack by the JNA and the Serb paramilitaries. However, the Croat-Moslem alliance did not last long. The Bosniak Moslems were upset and alarmed by well-documented reports (and subsequently fully confirmed) of talks between Milošević and Tuđman about a partition of Bosnia between Croatia and Serbia. There was, therefore, plenty of combustible material lying about waiting to ignite a full-scale war between the Bosnian Croats and Moslems. Both had, by the end of 1992, found themselves squeezed by the Serb offensive into less than 30 per cent of the republic's territory, though making up nearly two-thirds of its population (61 per cent according to the 1991 census). Tension between the two groups had begun to increase in the second half of 1992 as more and more mainly Moslem refugees, driven out by the Serbs from their homes in eastern and north-western Bosnia, poured into what had been ethnically compact Croat areas in the south of the republic, close to the border with Croatia.

Open Croat-Moslem conflict was sparked off by the publication of Western proposals—the so-called Vance-Owen plan, named after Lord Owen and Cyrus Vance, the chief Western negotiators at the time—for Bosnia's division into ten largely autonomous units or provinces under loose control of a government in Sarajevo representing the Bosnian Moslems, the Croats and the Serbs. For a whole year, that bitter war took the pressure off the Serbian forces. The Croat-Moslem war ended in early 1994 with near-total defeat for the HVO. The threat of international sanctions stopped Croatia from an open intervention to rescue the HVO. Under strong American pressure, an agreement was signed in Washington in March 1994 to set up a Croat-Moslem Federation in Bosnia and Herzegovina. The revival of the Croat-Moslem alliance transformed the political and military situation in the country. Instead of facing two adversaries destroying each other, the Serbs were confronted by a much more self-confident Bosnian army, not fully integrated with the Croat HVO but cooperating with it tactically in many areas. But both the Croats and, especially, the Moslems lacked the heavy arms with which to defeat the Serbs or at least push them towards significant territorial concessions.

By the middle of 1995 the Bosnian war had reached a military stalemate. Nobody had won, although clearly the Moslems were the biggest losers, in terms of territorial losses and personal suffering endured. By then the war in Bosnia had resulted in material devastation and human suffering on a scale not seen in Europe since 1945, with an estimated 100,000 people killed and more than 2 million rendered homeless. Even more than in Croatia in 1991, the Bosnian conflict saw massive application of the policy of 'ethnic cleansing'—forcible expulsion of (chiefly) non-Serbs from territories earmarked for Serb rule. In 1992 the UN's special rapporteur and Poland's former Prime Minister, Tadeusz Mazowiecki, laid on the Serbian force primary blame for the atrocities committed in Bosnia—notably the systematic rape of (chiefly Moslem) women and the killing and incarceration of large numbers of civilians in inhuman conditions. According to Mazowiecki's report, all sides in the war had committed atrocities but what marked out the Serb side was their scale and systematic nature. This led to calls by world figures for the setting up of war crimes tribunals modelled on that which tried Nazi war criminals in Germany after 1945. In May 1993 the UN Security Council made provision to set up such a tribunal at The Hague under the title of the International Criminal Tribunal for the Former Yugoslavia (ICTY). In July 1995 Bosnian Serb forces under the command of General Mladić outraged world opinion by occupying the UN-protected Srebrenica in eastern Bosnia and, in the worst massacre of the entire war in former Yugoslavia, subsequently killing some 8,000 Moslem men, whom they had taken prisoner.

In August 1995 the stalemate in Bosnia and Herzegovina was broken by several factors. The Croats had in the operations *Bljesak* (Flash) in May and *Oluja* (Storm) in early August of that year completed the recapture of the bulk of the territory that had been held by the rebel Serbs since 1991. An estimated 130,000 Croatian Serbs left hastily to Bosnia and Herzegovina and Serbia in an exodus organised by their own authorities. A joint Croat-Moslem offensive raised the siege of Bihać in western Bosnia. Croat and Moslem forces continued their advance into the heart of Serb-held territory in Bosnia and Herzegovina and occupied 23 per cent of it. At the end of August, NATO bombed Bosnian Serb gun-emplacements, ammunition stores and communication centres in response to the Serb shelling of a Sarajevo market called Markale in which forty-one civilians were killed and ninety wounded. The Serb collapse in Croatia and the successful joint Croat-Moslem offensive in Bosia and Herzegovina undermined Serb morale. Richard Holbrooke, President Clinton's envoy, mounted a mission, aimed at ending the conflict and re-constituting Bosnia and Herzegovina under a form of international tutelage as a single though de-centralised polity.

The Bosnian parties as well as the representatives of Croatia and Serbia and of the international community met in Dayton in the United States where a peace agreement was initialled on 21 November. It was signed in Paris on 14 December 1995. Under the Dayton Agreement, Bosnia and

Herzegovina was to have two Entities: the Croat-Moslem Federation, with 51 per cent of the territory, and the Serb Entity called *Republika Srpska* (RS), with 49 per cent. The tripartite presidency was to have a Moslem and a Croat member elected by the Federation and a Serb elected by the RS. The state was to have a small Council of Ministers, a Central Bank and a Constitutional Court. Military affairs, the taxation system and the judiciary were to be the responsibility primarily of the two Entities. A High Representative was to oversee the implementation of the Dayton Agreement on behalf of the international community, with the support of a 60,000–strong UN Implementation Force (IFOR). Elections were held on 14 September 1996, with Alija Izetbegović elected President.

Macedonia was the only constituent part of the former federal Yugoslavia to avoid military conflict that had engulfed the rest of it. Throughout the entire period of armed conflict following Yugoslavia's dissolution, Macedonia had a vital interest in the outcome, but little direct influence. In January 1991, following the first multi–party elections, Kiro Gligorov, a former top Yugoslav Communist leader, was elected President. Gligorov managed to persuade the representatives of Macedonia's ethnic Albanian minority (23 per cent of the total population, according to the 1981 census) to join the first multi–party coalition government. At a referendum held in September 1991 there was, on a 75 per cent turnout, a 95 per cent majority in favour of independence. Early in 1992, following the proclamation of independence in January, Gligorov negotiated the peaceful withdrawal of the JNA from Macedonia.

Macedonia failed to get the widely expected all-round immediate recognition by the member-states of the EU, due to Greece's objection that 'Macedonia' was a purely geographical term and that if a state called itself 'Macedonia' that would imply a claim on all the territory covered by the geographic term, and in particular the northern Greek province of 'Macedonia'. In February 1993 international arbitration produced a compromise name: 'The Former Yugoslav Republic of Macedonia' (FYROM). By the end of 1993 Greece was the only European Union member-state not to have recognised Macedonia. Following its recognition by Russia and the United States, Greece imposed trade sanctions against Macedonia in February 1994, but these were lifted in September 1995. Despite years of international mediation, the name issue remains unresolved as of end-2009.

3

THE ROAD TO RECOVERY AND STABILITY, 1996–2009

Managing political change in Albania, Bulgaria and Romania

Albania

By 1996, Albania appeared to be making a rapid transition to a market economy in the context of a stable political situation. However, the foundation for this was built on sand, and the country had to go through further convulsions before a new political maturity was found. The early warning signs appeared in the run-up to the 1996 parliamentary elections, when President Sali Berisha's Democratic Party of Albania (PDS) appeared to be losing support among the electorate. This drop in support was foreshadowed when a constitutional referendum, held in November 1994 with the aim of increasing the authority of the president, was lost with a clear 54 per cent majority for the opposition. This defeat led to further attempts to limit the opposition's freedom of manoeuvre. In September 1995, the parliament voted to lift the immunity of Zef Brozi, the head of the Supreme Court and parliamentary deputy who had opposed the constitutional reforms put forward in the November 1994 referendum. He was deprived of his passport, but American pressure and a prestigious award allowed him to leave for the United States. The jail sentence of Fatos Nano, the Socialist leader, who had been imprisoned in 1993, was further extended in order to keep him in jail when the elections took place. In September 1995 came the so-called 'genocide act' under which anyone who had held office in the Communist Party would be banned from public office till 2002.

The scale of the fraud as part of blatant government inter-ference in the first round of the election on 26 May 1996 led the Socialist Party (PSS) to refuse to take part in subsequent rounds. Berisha's Democratic Party, therefore, secured 122 seats against ten for the Socialists. Aleksander Meksi formed a new government, but its credibility was seriously damaged against the background of strong internal and international criticism. In early 1997, the collapse of a number of fraudu-lent speculative pyramid schemes sparked off a financial crisis that lost many thousands of people their savings and led to anti–government demonstrations (see Chapter V for more details). Those deteriorated into riots, looting and general breakdown of law and order. Nearly a million weapons were stolen from army arsenals and some parts of the country fell under the control of organised crime. A huge role was played throughout the year as well as afterwards by the international community in the re-establishment of law and order in Alba-nia, with Italy fulfilling a particularly important and construc-tive role.

The Meksi government was swept from power and replaced by one of national reconciliation under a Socialist, Bashkim Fino on 11 March 1997. New elections were held on 29 June and 6 July (with a third round in two constituencies on 13 July). The Democratic Party lost heavily with only twenty-nine seats against 101 for the Socialists under their party leader, Fatos Nano, who had emerged from prison. After the defeat of his party, Berisha resigned as President on 23 July and the Assembly nominated Rexhep Mejdani, a Socialist, in his place. Fatos Nano was made Prime Minister, a position he occupied until October 1998 and again between July 2002 and September 2005. In between, the country was ruled first by Pandeli Majko, and then by Ilir Meta who served competently as Prime Minister from 1999 to 2002. During his period in office he restored the government's control over most of the country, lost in the chaotic conditions prevailing in the aftermath of the total collapse of law and order in 1997. Meta continued to be undermined by Nano and eventually left the Socialists ahead of the 2005 elections to create his own party, the Socialist Movement for Integration (LSI).

Despite the improvements achieved during the Socialists' period in office, Albania's continuing reputation as a base for organised crime lost it some of the moral credit it had gained by temporarily accepting in the spring and summer of 1999 nearly half a million Kosovo Albanians expelled or fleeing from Kosovo during the emergency there. Albania not only accepted the refugees but also supported the NATO action in Kosovo. Western governments promised a reward for its cooperation including the prospect of an association agreement with the European Union, but those promises took a long time to fulfil.

The Socialists' long period in power ended in July 2005 with the return to office after a general election victory by Sali Berisha's Democratic Party. He had campaigned on a platform of fighting corruption. The Socialists had been badly damaged by their failure to tackle corruption as well as by their disunity. Following Berisha's election victory in 2005, his Democratic Party formed a centre-right coalition government with a number of smaller parties. Berisha's return to power provided him with an opportunity to show that he could govern successfully and thus wipe out memories of the disastrous collapse of his Presidency. Berisha made his party more inclusive by bringing in younger professionals and activists who had drafted much of the party's election manifesto. He also welcomed back former allies who had left the party in the 1990s in protest against his authoritarian style. Berisha's political position was strengthened by the election in mid-2007 of Bamir Topi, then deputy leader of the Democratic Party, as President. Berisha's PDS had thus captured the control of all the main public offices, but the opposition Socialists continued to enjoy considerable support, mainly in the rural areas and in the south of the country. They did well in the local elections in February 2007. Power shortages had harmed the PDS, which had, before returning to power in 2005, pledged to improve the electricity supply.

Parliamentary elections were held on 28 June 2009. All 140 members of parliament were elected through proportional representation from party lists in twelve electoral regions. It was a tight race between Berisha's Democratic Party (PDS) and the Socialists led by Edi Rama, the popular Mayor of Tirana, who was elected party leader on the platform of modernisation after his party's electoral defeat in 2005. Berisha's PDS won sixty-eight seats in a 140–seat parliament and was able to form a coalition government with the Socialist Integration Movement (LSI) of Ilir Meta, a former Socialist Prime Minister who later split off to form his own party. The Socialists won 66 seats and remained in opposition.

Albania's early support for Kosovo's declaration of independence (see below) on 17 February 2008 was widespread and bi–partisan. The Berisha government proceeded to forge strong links with Kosovo. Those include the building now in progress of a 250 km highway linking Priština with Durres on Albania's Adriatic coast. At the same time, the Albanian government and the entire political establishment has consistently gone out of its way to discourage speculation about 'Greater Albania'.

Bulgaria

The murder of former premier Andrei Lukanov on 2 October 1996 was an important event widely seen as a consequence of his threat to reveal the involvement of some leading Bulgarian Socialist party (BSP) figures in highly dubious or even illegal activities. The party had returned to power in a coalition with its smaller leftist allies, following its victory in the 18 December 1994 election. Zhan Videnov became Prime Minister in January 1995. However, the powerful commercial conglomerates, which had done well out of manipulating the subsidies to loss-making state enterprises, blocked attempts to end the subsidy system. Heavy bank lending to loss-making enterprises led in May 1996 to the collapse of confidence both in the banks and in the Bulgarian currency The international financial institutions, unhappy about the slow pace of structural reforms, refused to support Bulgaria's attempt to replenish reserves and called for a currency board to be established (see Chapter V).

Bulgaria at that time was on the verge of bankruptcy and was engulfed by a rising crime wave. Lukanov's murder did huge damage to Bulgaria and the Videnov government. The government's general ineptitude helped the SDS presidential candidate Petur Stoyanov to victory in November 1996. Videnov resigned as Prime Minister and BSP party leader on 21 December 1996. After an outbreak of violence outside the parliament building in Sofia on 10 January 1997, a wave of protests, strikes and blockades of major roads spread all over the country. Georgi Purvanov, the new BSP leader, refused to form a new government and a caretaker cabinet was formed.

Those events paved the way for the subsequent election victory of the SDS in 1997. The SDS secured 52 per cent of the vote and 137 seats in parliament. The BSP obtained 22 per cent and fifty-eight seats. On 19 May a new SDS government, under its leader, Ivan Kostov took office. Kostov introduced a macroeconomic stabilisation programme, which was based on a currency board, established in June 1997, with the Bulgarian leva pegged to the D-Mark. These steps and other measures succeeded in bringing down inflation from triple or even quadruple-digit levels in 1996–97 to 6.2 per cent in 1999. Bulgaria subsequently experienced robust economic growth. Under the SDS government, strong advances were made in structural reforms. The government took energetic action to combat organised crime and corruption. It tightened the laws on gun control, cracked down on criminal gangs and increased penalties for smuggling and tax evasion. In November 1997 the police service was reorganised and made more accountable to parliament. Penalties against other crimes were also increased.

The fight against organised crime led to tension with Russia. The government's expulsion of five foreign businessmen, four of them Russian, led to a quarrel, which reflected the Kostov government's generally cool relations with Russia. To reduce Bulgaria's dependence on Russian energy, the Kostov government sought to diversify its energy supplies. This fitted in with Bulgaria's increasing closeness to NATO. During NATO's conflict with Serbia over Kosovo in 1999, the government defied Bulgarian public opinion by allowing NATO the use of Bulgarian air space and denying Russia permission to fly over Bulgaria when it wanted to rush reinforcements and supplies to its troops at Priština airport towards the end of the NATO campaign. Bulgaria's agreement with Macedonia in February 1999, under which Bulgaria for the first time recognised the existence of a separate Macedonian nation, was followed by another on military cooperation in March. NATO welcomed both as a contribution to regional stability, though Bulgaria's progress towards both NATO and the EU remained slow.

The Kostov government's tough economic policies paid off. By the end of 2000 the currency had been stabilised and the country achieved a positive trade balance for the first time since the fall of Communism. However, the government's popularity suffered, due to continuing allegations of pervasive corruption and, perhaps even more, because of the high social costs of the reforms. The political situation changed dramatically in April 2001 as a result of the appearance on the political scene of exiled King Simeon II at the head of a populist movement, promising that he would carry out fundamental changes within 800 days of coming to power and including the total elimination of corruption. The elections on 23 June

2001 were won by the National Movement Simeon II (NDSV), set up in April 2001 and centred round the ex–King, who had recently returned to Bulgaria after a life-long enforced exile in Spain. The NDSV obtained 120 seats in a 240–seat National Assembly, the SDS got fifty-one seats and the Coalition for Bulgaria (KB), a grouping dominated by the Socialists, forty-eight.

Simeon's strongest political asset was the fact that, unlike both the BSP and the SDS, he was free from any taint of corruption and that, politically, he was not associated with either the SDS or the BSP. In July 2001 the former King, whose civilian name is Simeon Saxe-Coburg-Gotha, formed a coalition with the mainly Turkish MPS. The new, strongly reformist and pro-business government enjoyed international political and economic support. During its period in office, which ended in June 2005, it carried out many reforms and took Bulgaria into NATO and close to entry into the EU. However, the government's failure to meet its ambitious promises on economic prosperity and living standards led to a fall in the NDSV's support and to increasing divisions within it, which also weakened the government. The government incurred deep unpopularity because of a number of highly publicised corruption scandals and the continuing evidence of the power of organised crime.

Meanwhile, the Socialists continued to improve their position under their new leader, Sergei Stanishev, who had been elected in 2001, following the decision of the then party leader, Georgi Purvanov, to run for President and his successful election in 2001. The BSP emerged as the strongest party in the June 2005 elections, with 31 per cent of the vote and eighty-two seats in parliament. The NDSV obtained 19.9 per cent and fifty-three seats and the DPS 12.8 per cent and thirty-four seats. The BSP formed a coalition with the NDSV and the DPS. In the presidential election, held in two rounds in October and November 2006, Georgi Purvanov was re-elected for a second five-year term, beating a challenge from Volen Siderov, leader of the right-wing populist Ataka (NOA).

Although potentially a fragile alliance, the three-party coalition continued to function, driven by the national imperative to work together to get Bulgaria into the EU. The intensity of preparation for EU membership helped preserve unity within the ruling coalition. However, the NDSV was weakened by the formation after the 2005 election of a new political formation in parliament under the name of the Bulgarian New Democracy (BND) and made up of sixteen NDSV deputies who had left the party in protest against its decision to form a coalition with the BSP. The popularity of the NDSV has continued to decline since then.

Following a favourable European Commission report in September 2006, Bulgaria joined the EU on 1 January 2007. However, already in February 2007 the European Commission announced immediate and wide-ranging suspensions of pre-accession funds to Bulgaria amid concerns about corruption. Since then, internal divisions within the whole political establishment have increased and a newly formed, increasingly popular centre-right party emerged as the winner of the elections held on 5 July 2009. The party is called 'Citizens for European Development of Bulgaria' (GERB) and is led by the popular Mayor of Sofia, Boyko Borisov. GERB won 116 seats in a 240–seat parliament. On 27 July Borisov formed a coalition government with the right-wing Blue Coalition (fifteen seats), the populist Ataka (twenty-one seats) and the new Order, Law and Justice Party (ten seats).

In its 'benchmarking' report, published in July 2008, the European Commission criticised Bulgaria for making insufficient progress in reforming its judiciary and in pursuing the fight against corruption and organised crime. The EU withheld €500 million from its funding to Bulgaria and withheld the right to manage EU funds from two agencies in Bulgaria over corruption. The European Commission decided in November 2008 to cancel permanently €220 million in pre-accession funds and refused to unfreeze a further €300 million of pre-accession assistance. The European Commission has criticised the outgoing government for its failure to curb rampant corruption but has stopped short of suspending any further funds in addition those already cancelled in 2008. The European Union expects the new Bulgarian government to speed up the pace of judicial reforms and to deliver more results in the fight against corruption and organised crime. The July 2009 report noted progress in certain areas but stressed the need for further efforts to improve the judicial system and fight corruption and organised crime. EU monitoring of Bulgaria is to continue.

Bulgaria joined NATO in March 2004 and sent a peace-keeping battalion to the Polish-controlled sector in Iraq. The BSP opposed the decision and the battalion was eventually withdrawn in December 2005 to be replaced by a smaller unit to perform guard duties. Bulgaria has also contributed to the Western presence in Afghanistan. An agreement was reached on the establishment of American military bases in Bulgaria. Bulgaria's relations with Russia improved in 2001 after a period of coolness but in recent months Bulgaria has become the target of the Russian gas monopoly Gazprom's pressure to revise its contracts (Gazprom supplies about 90 per cent of Bulgaria's gas). Bulgaria maintains good relations with all of its immediate neighbours. Its relations with Serbia were not affected by Bulgaria's recognition of Kosovo's independence.

Romania

The November 1996 election was won by the Democratic Convention of Romania (CDR), the umbrella organisation for a number of centre-right opposition parties. The share of the vote by the CDR and its ally, the Social Democratic Union (USD), increased by 13 per cent while that of the Party of Social Democracy in Romania (PDSR) fell by 6 per cent. The CDR won 122 deputies in the lower house, the PDSR ninety-one, the USD fifty-three, the Hungarian UMDR twenty-five, the chauvinist Greater Romania Party (PRM) nineteen and the neo-communist Party of Romanian National Unity (PUNR) eighteen. A centre-right coalition government was formed by Victor Ciorbea, Mayor of Bucharet and a member of the Christian Democratic and National Peasants' Party (PNT-CD). With a 60 per cent majority in the lower house, Ciorbea announced his determination to break with Romania's Communist past and to crack down seriously on corruption. Ciorbea's economic programme was ambitious: elimination of price subsidies and controls on energy and foodstuffs, liberalisation of the foreign exchange markets and, speeding up privatisation and restructuring of the tax system. Ciorbea had little success and, having lost the support of a section of his own party, he resigned in March 1997. His successor as Prime Minister was Radu Vasile, whose policies were similar but who also proved ineffective. Vasile's government also became mired in intrigue and squabbles and he faced dissent and defections. In January 1998 the USD accused the Prime Minister of incompetence, inefficiency and ultra-conservatism. Vasile managed to stay in office until December 1998 when ministers belonging to his own party resigned. Meanwhile, output, real incomes and living standards had continued to fall.

In December 1998 Mugur Isãrescu, Governor of the Central Bank of Romania, who had a good record in defending the independence of the Bank and implementing the stabilisation of the economy in 1993 and 1994, was appointed Prime Minister. In January 1999 his government suffered a defeat in a confrontation with the miners. This harmed the government politically at home, but in December 1999 it scored a success in foreign policy when it received an invitation from the EU to begin accession negotiations in 2000. The poor record of successive centre-right administrations, both in domestic and in foreign policy, led to the defeat both of the Isãrescu government and of President Constantinescu in the elections of November 2000. The Social Democrats returned to power and Iliescu was re-elected as President for the third time in a run-off against Corneliu Vadim Tudor, leader of the ultra-nationalist Greater Romania Party (PRM), the second largest party in parliament. From 2000 to 2004, the minority Social Democratic government governed with the support of the ethnic Hungarian party UMDR.

At first, the Social Democrats enjoyed high levels of support. The government oversaw Romania's entry into NATO in March 2004. It was a reward for the support it had given in 1999, while still only a candidate for membership, to the NATO campaign against Serbia over the Kosovo issue. Towards the end of the Kosovo conflict, Romania had, like Bulgaria, forbidden Russian overflights to Kosovo where Moscow wanted to send reinforcements and supplies to its forces that had occupied Priština airport. The government's domestic support began to decline in 2004 reflecting the voters' increasing disenchantment with the huge scale of corruption and a spate of scandals involving the government's senior figures.

The centre-right coalition regained confidence, united and successfully challenged the Social Democrats in the elections in November 2004. Nevertheless, the Social Democrats managed to win the parliamentary elections, though with a small margin. However, the surprise victory of Traian Băsescu, leader of the Democratic Party (PD) and former Mayor of Bucharest, in the second round of the presidential election in December 2004 changed the situation dramatically. He defeated the Social Democrat candidate, Adrian Nastase, who had been seriously harmed by well-documented revelations in the media about large-scale corruption involving both himself and his party. Băsescu's victory paved the way for the formation of a centre-right coalition under Calin Popescu Tăriceanu, leader of the National Liberal Party (PNL) as Prime Minister. Also in the coalition were Băsescu's Democratic Party (PD), the Hungarian ethnic party UMDR and the Conservative Party (formerly the Romanian Humanist Party). Like the previous centre-right coalition from 1996 to 2000, this one was also rife with internal conflicts, partly contained by the need to work together to join the EU. Once this aim was achieved on 1 January 2007 the coalition started falling apart. It broke up in April 2007, when the PNL expelled the

PD from the cabinet, forcing it to go into opposition, but managed to hang on to power with help from the opposition parties.

In January 2008 a merger of the centrist Democratic Party (PD) and the centre-right Liberal Democratic Party (PDL), a breakaway from the PNL, established the Democratic Liberal Party (PDL). The PDL is regarded as the creation of President Băsescu, though the presidency is politically neutral according to the constitution. Since losing the election in 2004, the Social Democratic Party (PSD) underwent a period of reorganisation, Mircea Geoană, a moderniser who had served as Ambassador in Washington, was elected leader instead of Ion Iliescu. The party linked up with the Conservative Party (PC), in reality (despite its name) a leftist political grouping, and together with it managed to get the largest share of the popular vote in the elections in November 2008. However, the Democratic Liberal Party (PDL) won the largest number of seats in both houses of the Romanian parliament. Only two other parties—the National Liberal Party (PNL) and the Hungarian Union of Democrats (UMDR)—crossed the parliamentary threshold along with eighteen seats occupied by representatives of the national minorities in the lower house. The PNL, which ended third in the 2008 election after the PDS and the PDL, held the balance of power between the PDS-PC alliance and the DLP, but its insistence on retaining the post of Prime Minister ruled it out as a coalition partner. In the end, the PSD-PC alliance formed a coalition government with the PDL on 22 December 2008, while the PNL and the UMDR went into opposition.

Emil Boc, the new Prime Minister, is a protégé of Băsescu. He is leader of the PDL and a former Mayor of Cluj. Mircea Geoană, who was Foreign Minister in the 2000–2004 PDS government, occupies the important position of Speaker in the Senate (the upper house). The Boc government commanded a large majority (324 against 135 in both chambers). Unlike the previous administration, it was supported by President Băsescu. However, there was plenty of scope for conflict because of the deep differences between the two parties over economic policy and judicial reform. The presidential election later in 2009 resulted in Băsescu's re-election and the formation of a PDL-UMDR minority government coalition, again under Boc.

Romania joined the EU on 1 January 2007 but, like Bulgaria, was warned by the European Commission in all four of its post-accession reports to date of the need for stepped-up efforts to fight corruption. The July 2008 report singled out for criticism the judicial authorities' failure to initial prosecution proceedings against some top-level politicians. The government's stand on judicial reform and the fight against corruption as well as fiscal policy will determine future relations with the European Union. Romania avoided the imposition of sanctions following the publication of a critical European Commission report in February 2009, possibly because a new government had just taken office. A general report on fraud and irregularities with EU money in 2008 published in July 2009 showed Romania with the highest number of potential fraud cases from pre-accession funds. The European Commission did not accept the Romanian plan for an 'exit strategy' from the so-called cooperation and verification monitoring mechanism established when Romania joined the EU in 2007. As in Bulgaria, the July 2009 report noted progress in some areas, but emphasised the need for further efforts to reform the judicial system and to combat corruption.

Serbia on the road to change

On 27 April 1992 a 'rump' Yugoslavia was re-established by Serbia and Montenegro in the shape of the Federal Republic of Yugoslavia (FRY). Despite their active involvement in the wars in Slovenia, Croatia and Bosnia, neither Serbia nor Montenegro had experienced military operations on their own territory, nor had either of them faced any danger of military intervention from any outside quarter. Unlike in the Cold War period, none of the Western Powers had a strategic interest in the region and, therefore, they lacked the incentive to intervene in the military conflicts in the region. However, all found themselves under growing pressure from their domestic public opinion to try and stop the military conflicts and to punish those responsible for the atrocities committed on the ground. (See Chapter IV below for a more detailed analysis of the international community's policy towards the region—especially that of the European Community (EC), forerunner of the later European Union (EU).)

The Western governments' answer to this dilemma was the imposition in May 1992 of economic sanctions against the FRY. The rationale for this policy, which was a continuation of the generalised arms embargo imposed by Western governments in 1991, was the expectation that exposing the local population to economic hardship brought on by sanctions would help turn the public against the Milošević regime, and perhaps even cause its fall. However, the collusion both of governments and of business in the FRY's neighbourhood and beyond ensured that the sanctions proved ineffective. Rather than undermining the Milošević regime, they helped it increase its hold over the population by strengthening nationalist sentiment and the feeling of besiegement as well as hostility towards the West. Also, the shortages and inflation gave the government extra power to allocate scarce resources and decide, for example, which firms would get subsidies and which workers would, therefore, lose their jobs. It depended on the government whether old-age pensioners, veterans, farmers and soldiers would be paid. To guard against public unrest, Milošević increased by 20,000 the number of policemen in 1992 and strengthened special anti–riot police units. Perhaps the most negative long-term consequence of the sanctions was the creeping, gradually to become all-pervasive, criminalisation of the country's economy and the public administration. The vast network of criminals and corrupt officials and politicians that had sprung up to circumvent the sanctions regime not only benefited from it but also had a strong interest in seeing it continue.

Hopes for a political change in Serbia were raised in November 1996 when the opposition won the local elections in Belgrade and thirteen other cities. The ruling Socialist government's refusal to recognise the results led to three months of constant demonstrations. In the end, Milošević conceded most of the opposition's demands, but later he withdrew, one by one, the concessions he had made and sabotaged the implementation of others. His main success was the split in the opposition *Zajedno* (Together) coalition. One of the parties, the Serb Renewal Movement (SPO), led by Vuk Draško-vić, formed a *de facto* coalition with Milošević. In July 1997 Milošević, whose second and last term as Serbia's President had expired, was elected President of Yugoslavia by the federal parliament, which was made up of Serbian and Montenegrin deputies. Meanwhile, his attempt to have a safe successor elected as President of Serbia faced difficulties initially but, eventually, Milošević got his man: Milan Milutino-vić, Yugoslavia's Foreign Minister and Ambassador to Greece, was elected on 21 December 1997, beating Vojislav Šešelj, the leader of the ultra-nationalist radicals, who came second.

In March 1998, Milošević asked Šešelj, who had helped—with Belgrade's approval—to organise the 'ethnic cleansing' of Croats and other non-Serbs in Croatia in 1991 (and later that of Croats and Moslems in Bosnia and Herzegovina), to join the Serbian government. Šešelj's party was allocated fifteen of the thirty-six posts in the government, including the Ministry of Information, with Šešelj one of the deputy prime ministers. However, two internal crises, threatening the political *status quo* in FRY but also the stability of the whole region of South-Eastern Europe, began to build up in 1997, one of them in Montenegro and the other in Kosovo.

The crisis in Montenegro began in 1997 when Prime Minister Milo Đukanović, an erstwhile ally of Milošević, gained control of the ruling Democratic Party of Socialists (DPS) and beat the pro-Milošević President, Momir Bulatović, in that year's presidential election. There were several reasons for the evident anti–Milošević and anti–Belgrade backlash. Hopes of injections of financial aid from Belgrade, originally helpful to pro-Milošević forces, remained unfulfilled. Serbia was burdened by the huge cost of financing the wars in Croatia and Bosnia and Herzegovina and was unable to deliver. Economic sanctions against FRY hurt Montenegro's economy (though profits from contraband goods like oil and cigarettes imported into Serbia via Montenegro helped cushion the blow). The collapse of the Greater Serbia project also ended the dream shared by many Montenegrins of gaining the city of Dubrovnik on the Croatian Adriatric coast. In short, the Serbian link, which in 1989 had seemed to many Montenegrins a lifeline, had in the meantime become a bind. This had led to the regrouping of political forces, resulting in a rapprochement between the disenchanted section of the ruling DPA led by Đukanović and the opposition Liberals. Đukanović's new orientation attracted the votes of the section of the population interested in economic reforms promised by him as well as those of the small but electorally significant Albanian and Moslem minorities. From then on, Montenegro began to assert itself and simultaneously to distance itself from Belgrade over a variety of issues, including its Serbian nationalist legacy, war crimes and anti–minority policies.

The Kosovo conundrum

The crisis in Kosovo began also in 1997 when almost a decade of passive, Gandhi–style resistance to the Serbian occupation led by Ibrahim Rugova, ended in a complete stalemate. There had been some hopeful developments in 1996, notably a dialogue between Priština and Belgrade on how to solve Kosovo's education problem. The discussions, mediated by the Italian Catholic community St Egidio, resulted in an agreement signed by Milošević and Rugova in September 1996 to normalise the education system for Albanians in Kosovo. But the agreement was never implemented by Belgrade. In the eyes of the more activist Albanians, that setback was the final proof of the futility of Rugova's tactics towards Belgrade.

Then, in the second half of 1996, Milošević started showing himself weak in the face of the opposition's large-scale demonstrations and being obliged to accept the results of the local elections his party had lost. This helped both to radicalise the frustrated Kosovo Albanians and to give them new hope.

The Kosovo Liberation Army (UÇK), a small émigré group founded in the mid-1990s in Switzerland, carried out sporadic attacks on Serbian police in Kosovo in pursuit of its objective of an independent Kosovo. The collapse of law and order in Albania in March 1997 (see above) gave the UÇK access to weapons looted from Albanian army arsenals. The Serb police began to target UÇK activists and civilian sympathisers. In February and March 1998 there was an escalation of violence in Kosovo. The killing by the Serbian security forces in March 1998 of the entire large family (including women and children) of a UÇK leader produced a groundswell of support for the UÇK in Kosovo and improved its fundraising abroad. It also finally and firmly placed Kosovo on the international agenda. As Belgrade's repression in Kosovo intensified, so did the international demands, accompanied by threats of force by NATO and by the re-imposition of a variety of (mostly ineffective) international sanctions. By July 1998 the UÇK had gained control over large areas of Kosovo. A Serb counter-offensive in August led to 250,000 civilians being displaced. On 23 September 1998, UN Security Council Resolution 1199 called upon all parties to cease hostilities and, in particular, for the FRY to 'cease all action by the security forces affecting their civilian population'.

In October 1998, Richard Holbrooke, President Clinton's envoy, visited Belgrade, while at the same time NATO issued an Activation Order for air strikes to compel Milošević to come to the negotiating table. Following Milošević's agreement to the setting up of the Kosovo Verification Mission (KVM) that would check Belgrade's compliance with Security Council Resolution 1199 and the signing of a cease-fire, the NATO Activation Order was suspended. However, the cease-fire soon broke down, with both UÇK attacks and Serb reprisals continuing. In January 1999, following a massacre by Serb forces at Račak, NATO re-activated its air strikes Activation Order. Belgrade was issued by the Contact Group (Britain, France, Germany, Italy, Russia and the United States), which had for some years been dealing with the region, a package of 'non-negotiable principles' under the title of Status Quo Plus, which included the restoration of Kosovo's pre-1990 autonomy within Serbia, the introduction of democracy under international supervision, a commitment to stop all offensive action and repression in Kosovo, the safe return of persons displaced in the Račak area, and steps to avoid further humanitarian catastrophe.

Against the background of escalating fighting in Kosovo and an increasing exodus in early 1999 of ethnic Albanians into Albania, Macedonia and Montenegro, a peace conference, chaired jointly by Britain, France and Russia, was convened in Rambouillet near Paris on 6 February 1999. The conference was to define the terms of an agreement providing for a cease-fire, a peace settlement and the deployment of an international peacekeeping force within Kosovo to uphold that settlement. Milošević stayed away and sent the President of Serbia, Milutunović, instead. The Albanian side had two key demands: a binding referendum on independence after a three-year interim period and a NATO ground force in the meantime. The Serb side rejected any return to the pre-1990 situation as well as any international role in the governance of Kosovo. Desperate to avoid making good their threat through NATO to use force against Serbia, Western governments agreed to the extension of the conference by a month. On 23 February Britain and France announced a broad compromise. By 18 March the Albanian delegation had signed the draft agreement. On 23 March the Serb Assembly in Belgrade accepted the principle of autonomy for Kosovo and other non-military parts of the draft Agreement, but rejected as 'occupation' the idea of a military peacekeeping force in Kosovo.

On 24 March 1999 NATO started its bombing campaign, which lasted till 9 June. One of the important though unspoken motives for the West's intervention in Kosovo was undoubtedly a sense of guilt and a determination not to allow another humanitarian disaster like Bosnia to happen. The other was the realisation that NATO's credibility was at stake. The choice of air strikes was widely criticised as both inappropriate and inadequate but, with military intervention with ground forces ruled out, it was chosen as the next best option. The NATO campaign had three basic aims, popularly defined as 'Serbs out, peacekeepers in, refugees back'. It achieved them all. Serbia withdrew its security forces, which NATO bombing had barely touched, though NATO bombs had destroyed a lot of Serbian infrastructure (bridges on the Danube, power stations, oil refineries, TV installations and so on). The number of casualties, both military and civilian, still remains contested.

The international debate about what made Milošević decide to withdraw from Kosovo in June 1999 still goes on. It is argued by some that he feared that, despite the well-known resistance within the Western Alliance to a NATO ground force offensive to follow the air strikes, such an offensive might in the end have taken place, escalating into a full-scale war and resulting in Serbia's defeat and military occupation on the model of those after the Second World War in Germany and Japan. Others see Russia's role as decisive. They speculate that, though clearly unwilling to back Milošević to the hilt, the Russians may have offered him a face-saving compromise in the shape of a Russian occupation zone in northern Kosovo that could be kept warm by the Russians for eventual handover, in the fullness of time, to Serbia. Of course the Russian plan, if it did indeed exist, came to nothing, because the Russians did not get an occupation zone in Kosovo. What, however, gives this hypothesis some credence is the spectacular rush by Russian forces stationed in Bosnia and Herzegovina across Serbia to Slatina Airport in Priština in June 1999, which they managed to get to and temporarily secure before surrendering it to NATO forces.

Under UN Security Resolution 1244 adopted in June 1999, Kosovo was placed, as a *de facto* protectorate, under a body called the United Nations Interim Administration Mission in Kosovo (UNMIK), with a largely NATO force ensuring law and order and with the task of 'facilitating a political process designed to determine Kosovo's final status'. By November 1999, out of 848,100 ethnic Albanians who had been expelled by the Serbian security forces (or had simply fled), 808,913 had returned to Kosovo according to estimates from the UN High Commissioner for Refugees (UNHCR). Of the 200,000 or so Serbs and other non-Albanians who fled from Kosovo in 1999, few have returned so far.

After Tuđman and Milošević

In 2000, important political changes took place in Croatia and Serbia, making it a watershed year not only for those two countries but also for the rest of South-Eastern Europe.

Croatia

In Croatia, the death of seventy-seven-year-old President Franjo Tuđman on 10 December 1999 was followed by two important political events. The first was the defeat in parliamentary elections on 3 January 2000 of the HDZ, the party Tuđman had founded in 1989 and led until his death. The victor was the opposition Social Democratic Party (SDP) whose leader, Ivica Račan, had in January 1990 taken the League of Communists of Croatia (SKH) out of the League of Communists of Yugoslavia (SKJ) and subsequently, in May 1990, allowed free elections in Croatia. Those elections had resulted in a landslide victory for the HDZ and a defeat for Račan's party, which had meanwhile changed its name to that of the Party of Democratic Changes (*Stranka demokratskih promjena*). That was later changed into the Social Democratic Party (also with the initials SDP). The second important event in 2000 was the election in February of Stipe Mesić, in 1991 the last President of the collective presidency of SFRY and later, in independent Croatia, first Prime Minister and afterwards Speaker of Parliament. In 1993 Mesić broke with

Tuđman over the latter's collusion with Milošević in a policy aimed at partitioning Bosnia.

Under Tuđman, the bulk of the SKH political, military, police, economic and judicial nomenklatura had joined the HDZ, leaving only the reformists in the much smaller SDP led by Račan. As a former Tito partisan in the Second World War and later a senior JNA general, Tuđman originally belonged to the Yugoslav 'nomenklatura'. In the 1960s he clashed with the Yugoslav Communist Party leadership over a number of issues, most of them relating to Croatia's position within Yugoslavia. In the 1970s he was imprisoned. Under Tuđman, the HDZ introduced the semi–presidential system of government. Tuđman was elected President of the republic. The HDZ evolved into a broadly based national movement, whose ideology was an eclectic mix of nationalism, traditional Catholicism, populism and even socialism. Tuđman had taken in the old Party cadres so readily, partly because he needed them to run his new state in wartime, but partly also because he believed in a 'historic reconciliation' between the Communists and nationalists who had fought each other in the Second World War. This meant that, unlike in most other former Communist-ruled countries in Europe, there was no 'lustration' of former secret police informers and operatives in Croatia, except on ethnic grounds (the Serbs). The upshot was that a combination of old Communist and new regional (particularly Herzegovina Croat) networks was able to capture a strong position both in the state sector and the private sector of the economy. Tuđman himself encouraged the enrichment of individuals and families close to his regime. Privatisations were carried out in a non-transparent manner. However, the broad lines of economic policy were liberal-reformist and included a successful monetary stabilisation in 1993. The man primarily responsible for it was Borislav Škegro, Vice-Premier and Finance Minister under Tuđman from 1994 to 1999.

Tuđman enjoyed huge popularity in Croatia up to 1995, at least partly due to the fact that the county had been at war and parts of it were still occupied. The opposition was weak, not least because the HDZ controlled the state television as well as the bulk of the print media. This changed after the re-taking by the Croatian army and police in 1995 of most of Croatia's territories that had been under Serb control since 1991 and the subsequent peaceful, UN-supervised re-integra-tion of the rest. With the 'national mission' accomplished, there was stronger pressure for more democracy. But Tuđ-man resisted it and, for example, in 1995 replaced, one after another, no fewer than four democratically elected opposition figures elected for the post of Mayor of Zagreb, Croatia's capital. His explanation was that, for reasons of state, the opposition could not be allowed to take political control of the capital. The tampering with the electoral system included the granting of the vote in Croatia to the Croatian diaspora, including those Croats who had always been living across the border in the Herzegovina part of Bosnia. Since the bulk of the Herzegovina Croats were HDZ supporters, this measure created a permanent electoral reserve for the HDZ.

The opposition victory in 2000 was spearheaded by a coa-lition formed in 1998 between Račan's SDP and the Croatian Social-Liberal Party (HSLS) led by Dražen Budiša, a Zagreb University student leader in 1970–71, subsequently jailed for four years by the Yugoslav authorities. In 1991 Budiša had briefly served as a Minister in a national unity government under Prime Minister Franjo Gregurić. In the second round of the 2000 presidential election Mesić defeated Budiša. Rac-ˇan formed a centre-left six–party coalition which, in addition to the SDP and the HSLS, included the Croatian People's Party (HNS), the Croatian Peasant Party (HSS), the Liberal Party (LS) and the Istrian Democratic Alliance (IDS). The new coalition abolished the upper house of the Croatian par-liament, reduced the powers of the President, launched a series of reforms in the secret services, the police and the army and sought to diminish the influence of various war veteran and other bodies, which had been formed and subsi-dised by the Tuđman regime. Croatia's foreign policy chan-ged, with a new, more constructive policy towards Bosnia and the ending of financial and political support for the old pro-Tuđman Herzegovina Croat leadership. Relations with the European Union became warmer.

The coalition, which had started off by functioning quite well under the relaxed, consensual leadership of Ivica Račan, soon began to show cracks, partly due to personal clashes among individual party leaders but partly also due to ideological divisions. Among the government's successes was the large-scale road-building programme linking the Adriatic coast to the interior and the neighbouring states that gave a great spur to Croatia's tourist industry. The Račan government's biggest problem was the strong opposition from the extreme right, which was in open rebellion against the government's policy of fuller cooperation with ICTY at The Hague. The broad anti–Hague front included, apart from the HDZ, the extreme right-wing Party of the Rights (HSP), the Catholic bishops and most of the clergy, war veterans' organisations and some senior people in the army and the security services. There was even talk of a possible right-wing coup.

Račan's slow and hesitant response was put down by many in Croatia to his awareness that his Communist past made him politically vulnerable to the charge of lack of patriotism. President Mesić had no such qualms and adopted a much more robust approach. That included summary dismissal, in his capacity as commander-in-chief, of nine serving senior army generals who had openly challenged government policy over a number of issues. Those pressures culminated in a public meeting in Split in 2003 in favour of the fugitive Hague defendant General Ante Gotovina, attended by more than 100,000 people (many of them bussed in from Herzegovina). The government did not actually give in to those pressures, but its vacillating, often contradictory, stance over the issue of cooperation with ICTY spoilt relations with Western governments and slowed down Croatia's progress towards the EU.

At the parliamentary elections in November 2003, the HDZ emerged as the largest party, winning sixty-six seats in a 152–seat parliament, with the SDP winning thirty-five seats. Ivo Sanader, a former close collaborator of Tuđman and for a while Deputy Foreign Minister, who had in 2000 been elected as HDZ leader, formed a centre-right coalition with two small centre parties and the Pensioners' Party (HSP) but also taking in five MPs from the national minorities. He launched an opening towards the Serbian and other ethnic minorities. This was paralleled in foreign policy by an opening towards Serbia as well as Bosnia and Herzegovina in the context of a greater willingness to engage with South-Eastern Europe as a region. Sanader's strongly pro-EU and pro-NATO policy was welcomed in the West. The capture and arrest of the fugitive General Ante Gotovina in 2005 led to the re-opening of talks with the EU on Croatia's accession. At the elections in November 2007 the HDZ emerged as the largest party. Sanader formed a coalition with the Croatian Peasant Party (HSS), the Croatian Social-Liberal Party (HSLS) and the Independent Democratic Serbian Party (SDSS). Slobodan Uzelac, one of the SDSS leaders, became one of the Vice-Premiers. On 1 July 2009, Ivo Sanader unexpectedly resigned both as Prime Minisrter and as leader of the HDZ following a long-simmering conflict with the HDZ's right wing. Jadranka Kosor, Vice-Premier in the outgoing government, was appointed Prime Minister on 6 July, having been elected by a show of hands at the HDZ party congress on 4 July. The composition of the government coalition remained the same as under Sanader.

Serbia

Between the Serb forces' withdrawal from Kosovo in June 1999 and the autumn of 2000, it became clear that, though things were going badly for Serbia, Milošević appeared to be succeeding in hanging on to power even after the debacle in Kosovo. For a while, indeed, it looked as if he might go on and on. Various pessimistic scenarios circulating in the West included: prolonged international isolation of Serbia; dra-

matically escalating impoverishment of the population leading to possible unrest; a military coup and, even, civil war.
However, those over-pessimistic predictions were proved
wrong. The victory in the Yugoslav presidential elections on
24 September 2000 went, not to the incumbent, President
Slobodan Milošević, but to Vojislav Koštunica, the joint opposition candidate. That victory, at first disputed by the Milos-
ˇević camp, was in the end confirmed with the help of growing
anti–Milošević protests. Those culminated in a mainly peaceful mass demonstration in Belgrade on 5 October that also
involved the ransacking of the federal parliament by the pro-
testers and the occupation of the state TV station. Koštunica's
victory in the presidential election was followed up by the
landslide victory of the 18–party alliance, the Democratic
Opposition of Serbia (DOS), in the Serbian parliamentary
elections on 23 December 2000. In January 2001, Zoran
Đinđić, leader of the Democratic Party (DS), a member of
DOS, became Prime Minister of Serbia. The DOS landslide
meant that the dismantling of the Milošević regime in Serbia
could begin

It was a formidable challenge. The heavy burden of the
past presented Serbia's new rulers with a number of urgent,
difficult problems, all of which needed to be tackled more or
less simultaneously. They included reviving a stalled economy,
restructuring Socialist-era industrial enterprises, tackling corruption and organised crime, bringing under control and
reforming the armed forces and the security agencies, and
dealing with the large number of ethnic Serb refugees from
Bosnia and Herzegovina, Croatia and Kosovo. The DOS coalition came from two constituencies. One consisted of those
who had made their first principled but unsuccessful stand
against the Milošević regime and its expansionist policy in
March 1991 and again (equally unsuccessfully) in 1996–1997,
and were now trying for the third time. The other, larger,
constituency consisted of those (including the highly influential Serbian Orthodox Church) who had turned against
Milošević, not because he had tried, but because he had failed

to achieve a Greater Serbia. Those two camps came together in the early autumn of 2000. However, there still remained the question of what tactic should be adopted to remove the regime.

The opposition leaders opted for political, non-violent electoral means, well aware of the existence of the still intact, well-paid security apparatus available to the (admittedly embattled) Milošević, and anxious to avoid bloodshed. This decision was discreetly but firmly backed by Western governments and NGOs, which had from mid-1999 substantially stepped up their aid for democratic change in Serbia. As part of this consensual, evolutionary approach adopted by the leaders of the political opposition, the DOS bloc actually made, during the crucial period between 25 September and 5 October 2000, a deal with the erstwhile staunchest supporters of the Milošević regime (army, police, and close political associates). Those groups were united in one aim: that there should be no future for Serbia without them. It was ultimately this 'alliance of elites' that, with strong Western support, carried out Milošević's non-violent removal from power. There was a price to be paid for this 'negotiated change', as subsequent events were to show.

It was obvious from the start that Serbia's extremely complicated political and economic circumstances in October 2000 required broad unity, under strong leadership, among the reforming part of the political class. In this respect, unfortunately, Serbia was from the start handicapped by the fact that the two main political protagonists of the new course were also bitter political rivals. In Đinđić, the country got an energetic, forward-looking reformer, with the right skills for the job and a determination to see it through. Vojislav Koštunica, a more laid-back figure, had as President of FRY no operational control over either Serbia or Montenegro (the latter had assumed full control over the republic's territory, except over the armed forces and the air traffic authority, in the last phase of the Milošević era). But Koštunica retained considerable influence as head of the Yugoslav armed forces.

Between Đinđić and Koštunica there was an intense personal rivalry. The two men had, jointly with a number of other political figures, founded the opposition Democratic Party (DS) in 1989, but in 1992 Koštunica had split off to found the Democratic Party of Serbia (DSS), a democratic party but with a strongly nationalist agenda. In 1996 the DS and the DSS joined a new opposition bloc called *Zajedno* (Together) but remained ideologically and politically far apart. Nevertheless, after the Serb withdrawal from Kosovo in June 1999, the Đinđić-Koštunica tandem was pushed to the top of the Serbian opposition, largely due to the efforts of Western (especially British) diplomacy, which was by then involved in direct promotion of democratic change in Serbia. Koštunica, though less well known, became the presidential candidate. The main reason was that Đinđić, whom Milošević tried to have killed (and who was therefore obliged to flee to Montenegro during the 1999 NATO bombing campaign), was mistrusted by nationalist Serbs. Đinđić was seen by Western diplomacy as the indispensable dynamic pro-Western and pro-market reformer. However, the West opted for Koštunica as its choice to beat Milošević in a direct fight. The reason was that, though Koštunica had not done much during the Milošević years (and had actually been tolerated by Milošević), he had impeccable nationalist, and even anti–Western, credentials and so could be relied upon to prise the bulk of the conservative, nationalist Serbs out of the Milošević bloc.

This new proactive Western policy towards Serbia represented a big change. For most of the previous decade (see Chapter IV below), Western governments could not quite decide whether Milošević was part of the problem or part of the solution to the crises in South-Eastern Europe, with most of them inclining to the more positive assessment. During the escalating conflict in Kosovo, and especially after it, the Western powers adopted an imaginative twin-track approach, aimed at isolating the Milošević regime and at the same time encouraging economic and democratic reform in Serbia. In addition to the arms embargo, a freeze on funds and an oil embargo, the EU imposed tight financial and visa restrictions on individuals linked to the Milošević regime. To minimise the impact of sanctions on the general public and to show the West was anti–Milošević but not anti–Serb, various humanitarian exemptions were introduced including the supply of fuel oil to municipalities under the control of the democratic opposition. Kosovo and Montenegro were exempted from the oil embargo and from some of the financial sanctions. As an incentive to the Serbs to embrace democracy, the EU and the US indicated that real democratic change in Belgrade would bring about the lifting of sanctions and the end of Serbia's international isolation. This chimed in with the Serbs' desire to return to normality. In addition, Western governments and NGOs helped the democratic opposition through a variety of programmes, workshops, seminars and training programmes abroad for opposition activists. Direct Western help to the independent media helped to offset Milošević's control of the state media.

That positive, supportive Western policy continued and was further fleshed out after 5 October 2000, the day Milošević was overthrown. Unfortunately, in the aftermath of Milošević's fall, it gradually became clear that, even with him no longer in power, Serbia was failing to make a clean break with his heritage and that change was going to be less radical than had been expected by Western government as well as by reform-minded Serbs. Many Serb democrats all too readily accepted the Milošević-era mantra that all the country's problems had been caused by a decade of wars and, even more, by international sanctions and by NATO's bombing campaign in 1999. With none of those factors operative after 2000, many Serb democrats showed little enthusiasm for reforms and, on many occasions, actually blocked them. For example, Koštunica withdrew his DSS ministers from Đinđić's coalition government in August 2001, accusing the government of not doing enough to combat organised crime. Afterwards, the DSS *de facto* became a part of the opposition, which also included Milošević's Socialists (SPS) and Šešelj's Radicals

(SRS). Milošević himself was arrested on 1 April 2001 and extradited, as an indicted war criminal, to the International Criminal Tribunal for the Former Yugoslavia (ICTY) at The Hague on 28 June 2001. His extradition pleased Western governments, but caused a strong backlash in Serbia

The backlash was chiefly directed against Đinđić. He had never been particularly popular in Serbia, but his public-opinion ratings plummeted following Milošević's arrest and extradition. Though the whole government took the decision, Đinđić was the one who was blamed. (Koštunica showed his personal disapproval of the extradition by publicly distancing himself from it.) Đinđić was perceived as kow-towing to the same West that had recently bombed Serbia and planning to deliver as war criminals to The Hague, in addition to Milošević, many military, police and civilian personnel involved in the wars in Bosnia, Croatia and Kosovo. To upset the anti–Hague lobby, a large and influential constituency, was bad enough. Towards the end of 2002 he challenged another, equally dangerous constituency by announcing that his government was setting up institutions to combat organised crime, corruption and the grey economy. Legislation had been prepared to introduce special courts to deal with organised crime and war crimes, and special prosecution procedures and witness protection programmes had been approved by the Serbian Assembly. In January 2003 the heads of the Serbian secret services were changed in preparation for the big crackdown. The army was scheduled to be put under full civilian control.

On 12 March 2003 Đinđić was assassinated in the forecourt of the government building in Belgrade. The violent removal from the political scene of this remarkable leader, who was the main driving force of political and economic reform, left a huge gap. However, the initial response of the post-Đinđić Serbian government under Zoran Živković as Prime Minister was rapid and strong, Following a declaration of the state of emergency, the police began a large-scale operation, codenamed *Sablja* (Sabre), aimed at hunting down those responsible for ordering, planning and carrying out the murder. The initial target of the crackdown was the organised crime group known as the Zemun Clan linked to the Red Beret special forces unit that had been active in the wars in Croatia, Bosnia and Herzegovina and Kosovo and was also known for its close ties both to government and to opposition political figures. The police quickly arrested or killed most members of the Zemun Clan. The Red Berets were disbanded. In the first month of the crackdown more than 10,000 people were brought in for questioning. In the course of subsequent interrogations and investigations, the police claimed to have solved twenty-eight murders, twenty-three attempted murders, forty-five extortion attempts, fifteen kidnappings and dozens of other serious crimes as well as breaking up Serbia's largest narcotics ring.

Operation Sabre showed that Serbia's police were capable of operating effectively against organised crime when there was political will to do so. But the speed with which so many high-profile crimes were solved also showed that much information had already been widely known in police and even government circles. The answer to the question why so many criminals had apparently been permitted to go on acting with impunity lay in the close links developed under the Milošević regime between the state security service, paramilitary organisations, politicians and war criminals. Those parallel structures had been left intact when DOS ousted Milošević in October 2000. It had taken the shock of the Đinđić assassination to motivate Serbia's leading politicians to begin to deal decisively with the Milošević-era parallel structures. However, it was to take four years for the perpetrators of Đinđić's murder to be brought to justice; on 23 May 2007 the Special Court in Belgrade sentenced all twelve defendants charged with Đinđić's murder to a total of 178 years of imprisonment.

Fairly soon after the state of emergency ended in 22 April 2003, the government appeared to be weakening on the battle against corruption and economic crimes. Đinđić's assassination had led to a dramatic increase in the popularity of the Democratic Party and its leaders considered calling an early parliamentary election in order to have its post-Đinđić mandate renewed. However, in the end they decided against it. Factional struggles weakened Zoran Živković, Đinđić's successor as Prime Minister and DS leader. The DS's attempts to cling to power after Đinđić's assassination as a minority government by manipulating (and even buying) votes led to a public backlash against the entire political class. This helped both Koštunica's DSS and the ultra-nationalist Radicals (SRS), whose vice-president Tomislav Nikolić was deputising for its leader Vojislav Šešelj, who had surrendered voluntarily to the war crimes tribunal at The Hague in February 2003 to answer war crimes charges. The small, technocratic-reformist G17 Plus party joined Koštunica's DSS in a systematic campaign of mud-slinging against the DS, whose leaders—including the late Đinđić—were demonised in the media and in the Serbian Assembly. As time went on, with Đinđić gone and no fresh mandate from the electorate, the reform drive in various key sectors of the state administration and the economy slowed down.

A general election was called on 25 December 2003 by Živković when it became clear that he could no longer hold the remnants of the old DOS coalition together and would be unable to pass the budget for 2004. The Radicals emerged as the largest party, with eighty-two seats in a 250–seat Assembly. Koštunica's second-placed DSS obtained fifty-three seats and the third-placed DS, with thirty-seven seats, went into opposition. After prolonged negotiations, a minority coalition government was formed in March 2004. It was headed by Koštunica as Prime Minister, with the reformist G17 Plus and the conservative-nationalist New Serbia-SPO group as the junior partners. However, for its majority in the Serbian Assembly, Koštunica's coalition was obliged to rely on the Socialist Party of Serbia (SPS), founded by Milošević and still linked to him. For its part, the DS made it known that it would support, on an *ad hoc* basis, such legislation as it considered reformist in character. Much drama and controversy surrounded the election of the President of Serbia to replace Koštunica, who had become Prime Minister of Serbia in March 2004. Two attempted elections in 2004 failed, due to failure to reach the 50 per cent plus threshold. Finally on 27 June 2004 Boris Tadić, leader of the opposition Democratic Party since February 2004, who had served as Minister of Defence for Serbia and Montenegro from March 2003 to April 2004, was elected President for a five-year term in a tense runoff against Tomislav Nikolić, the Radical candidate.

Montenegro came to occupy much time and energy of Serbian politicians in the post-Milošević period. The need to redefine the relations between Belgrade and Podgorica became urgent when, in 2001, Montenegro's President, Milo Đukanović, declared his intention to move towards independence by calling a referendum. Reflecting the growing mood of indifference towards Montenegro in Serbia, Serbia's top leadership, with the exception of FRY's then President, Vojislav Koštunica, agreed that Montenegro should be allowed to go ahead with its referendum to determine the future of the relationship. However, at that precise moment, the European Union stepped in with a warning that a hasty separation might endanger stability in the region. Some officials in Brussels, notably Javier Solana, the EU's senior foreign policy official, were concerned that this separation would bring Kosovo out of its post-1999 limbo and place the issue of its final status, still to be determined, on the international agenda. Others worried that an independent Montenegro would not be economically self-sustainable and could become dominated by organised crime. Still others feared that the loss of Montenegro, coupled with that of Kosovo, might radicalise Serbian politics and they thought Serbia might more easily accept the inevitable loss of majority-Albanian Kosovo if it was allowed to 'keep' Montenegro.

Under Solana's strong personal pressure, the so-called Belgrade Agreement was signed in March 2002. This was followed by the Constitutional Charter signed in February 2003, which set up the loose State Union of Serbia and Montenegro. The Charter replaced the former federal Yugoslav structures with a figurehead central government and parliament that lacked any real authority and was totally dependent on the governments of the two republics. It included a provision that after three years, i.e., in 2006, referendums could be held to determine whether a majority in either republic wished to continue to stay in the Union. Neither of the republics liked the Charter. Serbia wanted a stronger, more centralised system, while Montenegro wanted complete independence and, therefore, resisted all attempts at forming an effective and functional central Union government. For Serbia, one of the most negative consequences was that, for a year-and-a-half during 2001 and 2002, Đinđić and his Ministers had to divert the government's priorities and resources away from the pressing political, economic, judicial and police reforms that had just been started in order to concentrate on the negotiations with Montenegro. This helped halt Serbia's reform process and gave the Milošević-era elements in Serbia time to regroup.

Not surprisingly, the plan to harmonise the economies of the two components of the Union in order to create a single market and customs area proved impossible to put into practice. This caused a lot of frustration on both sides, amid a growing sense that each could have advanced faster towards the EU separately rather than in the framework of the Charter. Eventually the EU itself recognised that the State Union was delaying progress towards EU integration. In September 2004 the EU Foreign Ministers adopted a twin-track approach—in other words, pursuing the integration process along separate tracks as far as technical, economic and administrative issues were concerned, while at the same time still officially endorsing the continued existence of the State Union itself.

In the end, both Koštunica and the EU reluctantly agreed to the holding of a referendum on independence in Montenegro on 21 May 2006. Turnout was 86 per cent and 55.5 per cent of voters (slightly more than the 55 per cent threshold insisted on by the EU) voted in favour of independence. Montenegro declared independence on 3 June 2006. On 12 June 2006 the EU Foreign Ministers recognised the referendum result and announced that EU member-states would individually recognise Montenegro. Diplomatic recognition from Serbia came on 15 June, following the Serbian Assembly's declaration on 5 June, that Serbia was the successor of the State Union. Montenegro became a member of the UN on 28 June 2006. Parliamentary and local elections on 10 September gave an overwhelming majority to Đukanovic's Democratic Party of Socialists (DPA). The anti–independence opposition bloc fared badly despite strong support from Serbia by Koštunica personally and his DSS, the Radicals, the nationalist intelligentsia and the Serbian Orthodox Church. Đukanović stepped down as Prime Minister in November 2006 but returned to office in February 2008, and convincingly won the parliamentary elections in February 2009.

The Kosovo endgame

The question of the final status of Kosovo, since June 1999 still *de jure* a province of Serbia but *de facto* a UN protectorate, did not dominate the political agenda in Serbia in the immediate aftermath of Milosević's fall from power in October 2000. There were, in the months immediately preceding Đindić's assassination in March 2003, reports of a deal over the future of the province being discussed by Đindić and Ibrahim Rugova, who was elected the province's President in 2002. However, nothing more was heard about the subject after Đindić's death. The international community seemed only too glad to leave the potentially explosive Kosovo final status issue on the back burner while Serbia and Montenegro were sorting themselves out. The official Western position was summed up in the so-called 'standards-before-status' formula, meaning that the issues of democracy, minority rights, law and order, privatisation and others had to be seriously addressed before discussions about the final status could begin

The respite bought by what was essentially a policy of Western procrastination was shattered by the inter-ethnic clashes that degenerated into anti–Serb and anti–UN riots in Kosovo from 17 to 19 March 2004. Those resulted in a number of Serb and Albanian deaths as well as substantial damage to Serb property and churches in Kosovo and the departure of thousands of Serbs from their homes. Those events occurred against the background of the Radicals' strong performance in the December 2003 Serbian parliamentary elections, the formation of a more nationalist government headed by Koštunica and much talk in Serbia about the need to 'recapture' Kosovo which raised among Kosovo's Albanians the spectre of a return to Serbian rule. Cooperation of the mainstream Albanian parties in Kosovo with the official UN 'standards-before-status' programme had left many Kosovo Albanians impatient and had created a political space for advocates of immediate, unconditional independence who were prepared to use violence to get it by pushing the Serbs out of Kosovo. Adding fuel to the fire was the frustration and anger among the young people of the province over the persistent heavy unemployment and the limited opportunities to travel to, and work in, the West that had been Kosovo's lifeline for decades.

Despite the fact that, inevitably, the public international response in the wake of the March 2004 riots had concentrated on not rewarding violent misbehaviour and emphasising continuity with the 'standards-before-status' policy, there was growing recognition both in Washington and EU capitals that procrastination over Kosovo was no longer an option. The nightmare scenario facing Western governments and the UNMIK administration in Kosovo was that, if the Kosovo Albanians' aspiration to independence was not seriously addressed, another bout of armed struggle threatening the stability and security of the broader region would be on the cards. This time, the target would not be the Serbian authorities but the UN and the very Western governments that had helped the Kosovo Albanians in 1999. In that sense, it could be said that the 2004 riots concentrated Western minds and pushed Western chancelleries into action. The united efforts by local Albanian party leaders in the wake of March 2004 to remove the bad image left by the riots by demonstrating clear willingness to make amends to the Serbs as well as, more generally, to ensure responsible and constructive behaviour by their constituency, helped persuade the international players that a solution for Kosovo was worth attempting.

The positive report presented in October 2005 by UN envoy Kai Eide on whether Kosovo was ready for the process of final status formed the basis for the authorisation, on 24 October 2005, by the UN Security Council of the appointment by the UN Secretary-General of the former President of Finland, Martti Ahtisaari, as Special Envoy charged with starting the political process to determine Kosovo's future status. The UN Office of the Special Envoy for Kosovo (UNOSEK), with Ahtisaari and his deputy, the retired Austrian diplomat and expert on South-Eastern Europe, Albert Rohan, was established in Vienna. Ahtisaari's independent position was confirmed by the so-called Contact Group, made of the key states interested in the Balkans: France, Germany, Italy, Russia, the United Kingdom and the United States The Contact Group issued in November 2005 a set of principles to guide the settlement of the status issue, emphasising that it should incorporate and promote, *inter alia*, regional stability and sustainable multi–ethnicity while rejecting unilateral steps and violence. However, the Contact Group did not provide a clear idea of where the process should lead ultimately.

Visiting Belgrade and Priština after his November 2005 appointment, Ahtisaari was confronted with two diametrically opposed demands. In Priština, it was the unanimous demand for an independent, sovereign Kosovo, while his interlocutors in Belgrade concentrated on tabling claims on property, assets, mines and mineral deposits in Kosovo and presenting a series of legal arguments for blocking independence. Ahtisaari's mission started against the background of growing international inclination to move towards monitored, conditional independence as the only realistic outcome. But while the Kosovo Albanians' priority was recognition of independence, with the difficult issue of decentralisation aimed at securing the remaining Serbs' rights coming second, the international community insisted on concrete plans and actions designed to accommodate the Serb minority. Serbia also wanted to see those issues resolved first. But there was a crucial difference here: the international community saw all that as opening the way for Kosovo's ultimate conditional independence, while Serbia saw each issue as a means of weakening Priština's control over ever more of Kosovo's territory and thus *de facto* undermining its viability as a future functioning independent state.

In the course of 2006, Ahtisaari and his team conducted several rounds of talks with Serbian and Albanian delegations in Vienna. Those ended, predictably, without a result due to the two sides' absolute refusal to deviate from their respective fundamental positions regarding sovereignty. Ahtisaari originally planned to present a blueprint he had prepared for Kosovo's final status to the UN Security Council in November 2006 However, the international community—or, more precisely, the EU—decided to see first what sort of government emerged from Serbia's important parliamentary elections on 21 January 2007. Those elections were held in the immediate aftermath of the referendum on 28 and 29 October 2006, which had endorsed Serbia's first post-Milošević Constitution. The main purpose of the new Constitution, which had been one of the most important electoral promises of Koštunica's DSS in the December 2003 elections, was to demonstrate Serbia's hostility to Kosovo's independence and to create further legal barriers against it. The Constitution makes it legally impossible—without amending the Constitution—for Serbia to recognise Kosovo's independence. At the referendum, the Constitution was endorsed by 51.46 per cent of registered voters (more than 95 per cent of those who actually voted), on a turnout of 53.6 per cent. The adoption of the new Constitution on 8 November 2006 was a victory for Koštunica's DSS as well as for the Socialists (SPS) and the Radicals. The biggest losers were President Tadić and his Democratic Party (DS).

However, the DS did relatively well in the 21 January 2007 elections, winning 22.9 per cent of votes and emerging second after the Radicals who won 28.7 per cent. Koštunica's DSS-NS coalition won 16.7 per cent of votes. Other parties that managed to pass the 5 per cent threshold and enter parliament were the liberal-technocratic G17 Plus, the Socialists and, to many people's surprise, Čedomir Jovanović's Liberal Democratic Party (LDP), which was founded only at the end of 2005. The nightmare scenario from Western governments' point of view—a coalition government led by the anti–Western and anti–reform Radicals—did not materialise. Four-month long negotiations over the formation of a new government had a negative economic impact, leading to hold-ups in structural reform and in the larger privatisations. Koštunica eventually took office as Prime Minister on 15 May, with the DS, now back from opposition, and G17 Plus participating in addition to his DSS-NS coalition. The broad division of responsibilities in the new government was that the DS and G17 Plus should handle the economy, foreign affairs and relations with the EU, while the DSS would be in charge of the Kosovo issue and that of cooperation with the International Criminal Tribunal for the Former Yugoslavia (ICTY). There was to be joint sharing of control over the security services.

The European Union, relieved over the exclusion of the Radicals from the government, immediately authorised the restarting of talks with Serbia about a Stabilisation and Association Agreement (SAA), which had been temporarily halted in May 2006 on the grounds of Serbia's insufficient cooperation with the ICTY. Once in the saddle, Koštunica's 'Mark 2' government mounted an all-out campaign against the Ahtisaari Plan for Kosovo, which had been unveiled in February 2007. This was despite the fact that the plan—full of 'creative ambiguity' (for example, it did not mention the word 'independence' nor did it mention Serbia's sovereignty over Kosovo)—allowed an extremely high degree of de-centralisation for the Serb minority in Kosovo and many other concessions. Kosovo itself was to be a *de facto* provisional protectorate, with eventual independence, under the supervision of an International Civilian Representative heading an International Civilian Office (ICO), mainly under EU control.

Serbia succeeded in derailing the original Ahtisaari plan. Russia provided strong backing for Serbia's position, with the implicit threat to veto the Plan if it should be submitted for approval to the UN Security Council. The Ahtisaari Plan effectively dead, the operational responsibility for the resolution of the Kosovo status issue was taken over by a 'troika' made up of Wolfgang Ischinger, German Ambassador to London on behalf of the EU, Frank Wisner, a senior State Department official on behalf of the US, and Alexander Botsan-Kharchenko, a high-ranking diplomat on behalf of Russia. The Western governments, especially those of the US and the UK, persuaded the Kosovo Albanians to postpone any unilateral moves pending the outcome of further talks about Kosovo's final status in late autumn of 2007. Serbia remained totally opposed to Kosovo's independence, though prepared to grant it wide autonomy. This was totally unacceptable to Kosovo Albanians who insisted on independence. The failure of additional talks between Belgrade and Priština with the 'troika' mediating, announced in December 2007, opened the way to Kosovo's unilateral declaration of independence, with the possibility of the Serb-majority northern Kosovo deciding to remain in Serbia.

With a big crisis over Kosovo looming and in an effort to help the moderate pro-reform forces in Serbia around President Tadić, who was seeking re-election in January 2008, the EU initialled the Stabilisation and Association Agreement (SAA) with Serbia in November 2007. However, the Netherlands made the signing of the SAA conditional on Serbia's full cooperation with the ICTY, including the extradition of General Ratko Mladić, former commander of the Serbian forces in Bosnia indicted for his alleged role in the massacre in July 1995 in Srebrenica, a UN-protected area at the time in the charge of Dutch troops. In the event, Tadić, who had trailed by almost 190,000 votes behind the Radical Tomislav Nikolić in the first round of the presidential election on 20 January, managed to defeat Nikolić in the run-off on 3 February by some 100,000 votes, on a high 67 per cent turnout.

Serbia mounted a diplomatic offensive aimed at preventing Kosovo from proclaiming independence and, if it did, punishing both it and the states ready to recognise it. Kosovo's 120–strong Assembly proclaimed independence on 17 February 2008. All 109 MPs present, including those representing Kosovo's non-Serb minorities, voted in favour. Serb MPs boycotted the sessions. The event took place in a peaceful atmosphere, with protests taking place only in the predominantly Serbian-populated north of Kosovo where the Serb MP's formed an illegal parliament. A huge protest rally in Belgrade on 22 February, addressed by many top Serbian political leaders (though not President Tadić), ended with groups of hooligans attacking Western embassies and looting the main shopping centre.

The question of how to respond to Kosovo's independence led to a deepening of divisions within the Serbian political establishment as a whole and the Koštunica-led coalition government in particular. The main split occurred over the pressure from the DSS, the Radicals and the rest of the so-called Patriotic bloc to make future Serbian progress towards the EU formally dependent on the annulment of the individual recognitions already made. That policy line was resisted by the Democratic Party, the G17 Plus and some other smaller parties, which argued that the European future of Serbia should not be made a hostage of the Kosovo problem. Divisions over tactics to be adopted towards the Kosovo problem led to the collapse of the coalition in March and the calling of parliamentary elections, at the same time as local elections, on 11 May 2008. The DS-led bloc 'For a European Serbia' did well, as did the small but strongly reformist and pro-European LDP, while the Radicals and the DSS did less well.

The Socialist Party, founded by Milošević, emerged as the kingmaker. The Radicals and the DSS tried and failed to form a coalition government with the Socialists.

On 7 July 2008 the Assembly endorsed a DS-led coalition government under Mirko Cvetković and including the Socialists and the representatives of national minorities. The LDP promised conditional support. The new government announced that entering the EU would be its top priority and initiated in parliament the process leading to the endorsement of the SAA agreement initialled with the EU in 2007. On 21 July 2008 the arrest of Radovan Karadžić, a top Hague indictee, who had been on the run for twelve years, was announced. On 27 July he was extradited to The Hague to be tried for serious crimes in Bosnia, a development warmly welcomed by EU and US governments though coupled with warnings that full cooperation with the ICTY at The Hague still required the arrest and extradition of two other indictees: Ratko Mladić and Goran Hadžić, head of the statelet comprising Serb-occupied Croatian territories in the 1991–95 period. Karadžić was put on trial in March 2010.

Serbia's fierce opposition to Kosovo's independence has slowed down but not derailed the process of Kosovo's recognition as an independent state. The threatened Serbian retaliatory measures against states recognising Kosovo have proved ineffective. They failed to deter such major would-be recognisers as the United States and, in the EU, France, Germany, Italy and the UK. The EU had, against the background of considerable internal disagreement, decided that states wishing to recognise should do so individually. Most have done so, with the exceptions of Cyprus, Greece, Romania, the Slovak Republic and Spain. Among UN members, the rate of recognition has been slow but steady. By January 2010, 65 UN members had recognised Kosovo. Meanwhile, Serbia has taken its case to the International Court of Justice, a move that has defused tensions somewhat for the time being.

With the road to UN Security Council approval blocked by the threat of a Russian veto, the EU and the United States decided to by-pass the UN and set up an International Steering Group (ISG) for Kosovo to manage the handover from the UN to the European Union as the supervisor of the newly-but-not-quite-fully-independent Kosovo. At its meeting in Vienna in February 2008, the EU approved funds, logistics and operational programmes for a 1,800–strong EU-led civilian force (EULEX) in Kosovo to oversee its independence. As a result of strong Russian opposition in the UN Security Council, EULEX was obliged to start operating in Kosovo still under UN authority. International assistance, including that from the EU, continued for the time being to be provided in a 'status-neutral' way.

4

THE EXTERNAL DIMENSION, 1989–2009

Fallout from the collapse of the Berlin wall

The governments of Western Europe and the United States were totally unprepared for, and in some cases not entirely pleased with, some of the consequences of the fall of the Berlin Wall and the subsequent collapse of the Communist regimes in Central and South-Eastern Europe. In Central Europe, they welcomed the end of Soviet domination over Czechoslovakia, Hungary and Poland as well as the exit of the three Baltic Republics from the Soviet Union. However, the French President, François Mitterrand, and the British Prime Minister, Margaret Thatcher, did not look with favour upon the rapid moves towards the unification of the Federal Republic of Germany (FRG) and the German Democratic Republic (GDR), which was being energetically pursued by the FRG's Chancellor, Helmut Kohl, and supported by President George H. W. Bush's Administration in the United States. Margaret Thatcher, in particular, worried that the emergence of a re-united Germany with 80 million inhabitants would produce a sudden change in the balance of power within the European Union and in Europe as a whole. Britain and France tried to slow down the process of unification but their attempt quickly ended in failure.

Western governments also welcomed the end of Soviet domination in South-Eastern Europe, and looked forward to the establishment of democracy, the rule of law and the free-market system in the region. Like in Central Europe, scores of Western consultants, some of them financed by the US and the EU and others by Central and East European diasporas in the West, descended on the countries of the region to help with the transition process. Numerous well-meaning, but not always sufficiently focused, NGOs became busy in the region. They sought to turn countries like Albania, which was emerging from decades of complete isolation, into laboratories of political, economic and social experimentation. Not surprisingly, the results were mixed, at least partly because the enthusiastic missionaries of transition did not always grasp two important things. The first was that the principal motive of the local populations in wanting change was to catch up with Western Europe's living standards as rapidly as possible. The second was that those same populations were unaware of the pain necessarily involved in the process.

Ironically, the only country in South-Eastern Europe that presented Western governments with a major and immediate policy challenge was Yugoslavia, which had in previous decades moved closest to the West and had received much help and encouragement from it for its attempts to reform itself, but which now looked in danger of disintegrating. Slovenia and Croatia, Yugoslavia's two westernmost republics, had started to move towards independence, having finally realised that a peaceful divorce on the model of the (much-studied) one between Norway and Sweden in 1905 would not be allowed by Slobodan Milošević's regime in Serbia and the Yugoslav People's Army (JNA). Those moves were backed by massive pro-independence referendums—Slovenia in December 1990 and Croatia in May 1991. However, individual Western governments and the European Union chose to ignore both those referendums and what had led to them and, while appealing to all the republics in Yugoslavia to strive for a peaceful settlement, they leant particularly heavily on would-be 'secessionists', Croatia and Slovenia. These republics were asked to reconsider their intention to declare independence and were told repeatedly by Western politicians that a cold welcome awaited them if they disregarded their pleas not to leave Yugoslavia.

With Croatia and Slovenia evidently in mind, President George Bush wrote in March 1991 to Yugoslavia's Prime Minister, Ante Marković, warning that the United States 'would not reward' those who split off from Yugoslavia without the agreement of all the parties involved. The warning was re-iterated in even blunter terms by the US Secretary of State, James Baker, in June 1991. During a brief visit to Belgrade en route to Tirana, he said that the United States would not recognise any unilateral declarations of independence by Croatia and Slovenia. Change could take place, he said, but only through dialogue among all parties and a final agreement among all of them. He emphasised that US policy supported a democratic, united Yugoslavia.

The EU (then still the European Community) followed the same line. On the eve of its ministerial meeting in Dresden on 13 May 1991, Austria's Foreign Minister, Alois Mock, suggested the setting up of a group of 'wise men'—independent experts whose task would be to help the Yugoslav republics settle their problems. This proposal was rejected, as was that by Catherine Lalumière, the then Secretary-General of the Council of Europe, for a mediation group to be drawn from among the experts within the Council of Europe. The UK Foreign Secretary, Douglas Hurd, who had placed Yugoslavia on the agenda of the Dresden meeting, suggested that Yugoslavia could be transformed into a 'loose confederation', but that outright independence for Croatia and Slovenia should be rejected. EU ministers decided to dispatch a delegation to Yugoslavia, consisting of Jacques Delors, President of the European Commission, and Jacques Santer, Prime Minister of Luxembourg. The message the delegation brought to Belgrade in May was that the EU was ready to offer aid and closer relations, including an Association Agreement, provided

Yugoslavia remained together and solved its problems within the following framework: a single market; a single currency and a central bank; a single army; a single joint policy-making mechanism; and a common system for the protection of human rights and ethnic minorities throughout Yugoslavia. An important though symbolic part of the mission's message, clearly aimed at the 'separatists' in Croatia and Slovenia, was its insistence on dealing solely with the federal government in Belgrade. It was with that government that the EU signed on 24 June 1991, the day before Croatia and Slovenia declared their independence, a five-year ECU (later Euro) 807 million loan agreement.

This gesture by the EU demonstrated a serious misunderstanding of the political realities in Yugoslavia. In the deadly political poker game between Belgrade on one side and Ljubljana and Zagreb on the other, financial inducements offered by outsiders, however well-meaning, could not any longer play a constructive and conciliatory role. The West's stance was, predictably, interpreted by the hardliners in Belgrade as a sign that the West would not stand in the way of their campaign of recentralisation. It could hardly be otherwise, in view of the fact that Western appeals for a settlement of the crisis without the use of force did not spell out what, if anything, the West would do to those who actually used force. Croat and Slovene leaders faced a choice between what amounted to surrender to Belgrade and a risky bid for independence. They opted for the latter because they sensed that the majority of Croats and Slovenes would not countenance any backing down under pressure of threats from Belgrade. But Serbia was in a confident mood and not at all ready to accommodate Croatia and Slovenia. A serious confrontation was looming.

Why did Western governments lean on the 'secessionists' alone? There was, first of all, an understandable reluctance to contemplate the inevitably messy and complicated break-up of a state into which so much Western money and effort had been poured since its expulsion from the Soviet bloc in 1948.

The EU, which had extended to Yugoslavia a high degree of preferential treatment since the mid-1960s, had convinced itself that its protégé was, by and large, a success story and a worthy candidate for early association and, eventually, membership. There was also a reluctance to face the new costs the EU would be likely to incur if Yugoslavia were replaced by a number of small successor states. Admittedly, the old fear that, if Yugoslavia became internally de-stabilised, the Soviet Union would move in and seek to take control had ceased to be a factor in Western calculations since the collapse of Soviet power in Eastern and Central Europe in 1989–90. However, there was a concern that the break-up of Yugoslavia would plunge the whole of South-Eastern Europe into a crisis by reopening a number of old territorial issues centring on Kosovo and Macedonia that had been settled after 1945. Beyond that there was the worry, both for the United States and for Western Europe, that if Yugoslavia disintegrated and Croatia and Slovenia became independent, a dangerous precedent would be set for the break-up of Czechoslovakia and of the Soviet Union, with many attendant nuclear complications in the latter. There was also the unspoken fear in some West European states that the break-up of Yugoslavia could encourage, and thus exacerbate, the already existing secessionist tendencies in Western Europe, notably in Italy, Spain, France and Britain.

In short, for the West what was happening in Yugoslavia in 1990–91 was, quite, simply, the wrong crisis (one of disintegration in an integrating Europe), at the wrong time (when the West had to cope with the consequences of Germany's reunification, the dramatic changes in the Soviet Union and the armed conflict in the Middle East), and in the wrong place (in South-Eastern Europe which had, now that the Cold War was over, ceased to be a region of high strategic importance). From that perspective, the *status quo* in Yugoslavia, however imperfect, looked vastly preferable to almost any alternative.

This 'pro-*status-quo*-come-what-may' policy, though perhaps understandable, was wrong, because it ignored the overwhelming evidence that the old Titoist order in Yugoslavia had irretrievably broken down. Those in the West backing the *status quo* in Yugoslavia were chasing a phantom. Given the irreconcilable differences between Croatia and Slovenia on one side and Serbia on the other, Yugoslavia could no longer be kept together except by force under a government propped up by strong outside political, diplomatic and, above all, economic support. Tito had had this support from the West during the Cold War years, but the Cold War was over and Western governments were no longer sufficiently interested in Yugoslavia to pay a high price for its continued existence. But those governments' perceptions were clouded, partly thanks to Ante Marković, the reform-oriented but politically naïve federal Yugoslav Prime Minister.

Marković held out to his Western backers the possibility of squaring all the conflicting interests within the framework of a radical economic and financial reform. What he was proposing was, in effect, an economic solution to what were essentially deep-seated political problems. Unsurprisingly, he was unable to fulfil his promise. Besides, he committed the tactical error of trying to buy support, first from Milošević by letting him overshoot Serbia's spending targets and thus giving him a chance to offer in Serbia large pre-election wage and salary increases; and second from the JNA by exempting it from drastic military budget cuts already agreed among Yugoslavia's political leaders. However, Western governments (particularly that of the United States) continued until the very end to display a seemingly blind confidence in Marković despite the poor electoral showing at the elections in the individual federal republics of the Reform Alliance, the party he had set up in 1990.

Dithering over collapsing Yugoslavia

The outbreak of war in Yugoslavia in June 1991 came as a shock not only for Europe but also for the rest of the world where Yugoslavia, its late leader Tito and its self-management system had many admirers. The armed conflict in Yugoslavia also posed a serious dilemma for Western governments. Was it taking place within a sovereign state and should it, therefore, be regarded as that state's internal concern? Or was it aggression by one state against another and, therefore, something that justified, possibly even demanded, an official response under the UN Charter? In legal terms, the issue was not simple. Slovenia had been attacked by the JNA two days after it had proclaimed its independence. However, from the international point of view, nothing had changed, because neither Croatia nor Slovenia had yet been recognised diplomatically as sovereign states, and they were not (yet) members of the UN. Therefore, officially they still formed a part of Yugoslavia, a sovereign state and a member of the United Nations. For their part, Slovenia and Croatia clearly regarded themselves already as sovereign states and looked to the international community both for diplomatic recognition and for support.

On the ground, the opposing sides justified their actions by reference to the 1974 Constitution. The JNA high command claimed that, in intervening in Slovenia against the local territorial defence forces, it was simply fulfilling its constitutional obligation to protect Yugoslavia's unity and territorial integrity following a demand from the federal Yugoslav government on 25 June for the 'repossession' from the Slovenes of Yugoslavia's international borders, which had been confirmed by the federal assembly in Belgrade. Slovenia claimed that, on the contrary, the JNA was impeding it in the exercise of its constitutional right, enshrined in the 1974 Constitution, to exit from the Yugoslav federation in line with the decision of the clear majority of its population democratically expressed at a special independence referendum. Furthermore, the Slovenes argued, it was not they but the JNA that was acting unconstitutionally and without legal authority in intervening in Slovenia. Authority for such action could have been given to the JNA only by Yugoslavia's eight-member collective presidency, in its capacity as the commander-in-chief of the country's armed forces. Only the presidency could order troop movements in any of the individual republics whose prior agreement in this matter had first to be obtained at the level of the federal presidency, by virtue of their status as states (*države*) and not mere administrative units. But the presidency had, since May 1991, been paralysed by the Serbian voting bloc's refusal to allow the routine election of Stipe Mesić, a Croat, as its chairman for the May 1991–May 1992 period.

The war in Slovenia in June 1991 set the alarm bells ringing in the West. The ink on the Charter of Paris, which had codified the norms of acceptable international behaviour in November 1990, was barely dry; it was impossible for governments simply to ignore the first war in Europe since 1945, especially when so many people were concluding that Europe had permanently banished the danger of war. Still, most governments, as is their wont, appeared be paying more attention to their own topical preoccupations than the dangerous situation on the ground in Yugoslavia. Who was to deal with the situation in Yugoslavia anyway was the question.

NATO was precluded, by its own rules, from participating in what was for it an 'out-of-area' conflict. However, NATO gave its permission for its members' navies to take part in joint maritime patrols with the Western Europan Union (WEU) off the Adriatic coast to monitor the arms embargo that had been routinely imposed by the UN shortly after the outbreak of the armed conflict in Yugoslavia. The 12–member WEU had been dormant since its inception in 1948 but had become more important in the late-1980s because some saw it as a possible defence arm of the EU. Later, NATO navies undertook the monitoring of the enforcement of the economic sanctions that had been imposed on the rump Yugoslavia (Serbia and Montenegro) in May 1992.

The Conference on Security and Co-operation in Europe (CSCE), which had in the late-1980s increasingly come to be regarded as a putative pan-European security system, demonstrated its severe limitations in the Yugoslav conflict. The

June 1991 meeting of the CSCE's Foreign Ministers in Berlin, held on the eve of war in Slovenia, expressed concern about the situation in Yugoslavia, the first time the 35 countries had issued an opinion on a member-state. But, once war had begun, there was little the organisation could do. Its conflict-prevention centre in Vienna, set up by the CSCE summit in Paris in November 1990 with the task of promoting confidence- and security-building measures, had been overtaken by the war. The CSCE's second available instrument, the emergency mechanism, was invoked by Austria and a meeting was held in Prague a few days after the war's outbreak. The meeting issued a call for a cease-fire and endorsed the sending of an EU monitoring mission to Yugoslavia. After thus additionally easing and legitimising the EU's formal entry into the Yugoslav crisis, the CSCE receded into the background as the EU took the lead.

For the European Union, the crisis in Yugoslavia was a headache but was also seen as an opportunity. The EU was in the middle of a debate about its future development, which centred on the subject of a common EU defence and foreign policy. Talk of a common foreign policy usually meant in practice that, in the interests of unity, joint foreign policy initiatives were reduced to the lowest common denominator. Debates about a separate European defence policy were aggravated by disagreements as to whether the aim was at all desirable in view of its possible divisive impact on NATO. In late July 1991, shortly after the outbreak of war, France proposed that a military intervention to stop the war should be undertaken by the WEU. There were, however, serious disagreements between the 'Atlanticists' (the UK, Portugal and the Netherlands) who saw the WEU simply as a handy 'European pillar' of the Atlantic Alliance, and others, particularly, France, who wanted to make it into a distinctive European defence organisation. The French July 1991 initiative came to nothing, but in September 1991, as cease-fire after cease-fire in Croatia broke down, the possibility of sending EU states' troops wearing WEU hats into Yugoslavia was raised again.

The renewed French proposal was supported by Germany, Italy and the Netherlands, but the UK opposed it.

After an argument between those, like France, who wanted to send in a force to establish the conditions of peace and those like Britain who (with Northern Ireland obviously in mind) argued that it would be irresponsible to send such a force into a country where there was no peace to be kept, the non-interventionists won. They were helped by two factors: the entirely predictable absence of an invitation for a WEU force from Serbia, and the British determination to nip in the bud the Franco-German idea for a Euro-army, with Britain likely to be the main contributor. Here, as on subsequent occasions, questions of more immediate political concern to EU members squeezed the situation on the ground in Yugoslavia lower down the list.

Having failed to stop the armed conflict in Yugoslavia, the EU was reduced to managing it. This happened in two ways: through arranging cease-fires on the ground; and through the Peace Conference on Yugoslavia, first at The Hague and then in Brussels. Both efforts failed. The only cease-fire successfully brokered by the beginning of 1992 was that by Cyrus Vance on behalf of the UN. The second session of the Peace Conference, hurriedly convened in September 1991 under Lord Carrington, proved to be little more than a talking-shop. It brought together the Yugoslav federal presidency, the federal government and the presidents of the six republics, but when Carrington suggested the establishment of sovereign and independent republics for those who wished it, Serbia rejected the proposals. The conference collapsed in November 1991 and the UN was brought in.

The United Nations, the body equipped with the right kind of international legitimacy and instruments and, therefore, best suited for action in that crisis, stood aside initially. It was only in November 1991 that the UN's first official contact with the crisis began when the UN Secretary-General, Xavier Peréz de Cuéllar, appointed Cyrus Vance, who had been US Secretary of State under President Jimmy Carter, as his special envoy to the mediation mechanism that had been set up by the European Union. The UN's direct and active involvement came in February 1992, when the Security Council decided to send a UN force, with a narrow peacekeeping mandate, to Croatia, which had become involved in the war after the end of the one in Slovenia.

By the beginning of 1992, the war in Croatia had reached a stalemate. The combined JNA/Serb paramilitary operations in various parts of Croatia had resulted in the occupation of about a third of the republic's territory and a cease-fire had been arranged, which the UN, in effect, came to police. Under UN Security Council Resolution 743, a body called the United Nations Protection Force (UNPROFOR) was dispatched to the so-called UN-Protected Areas (UNPAs)—mainly areas under Serb control at the time of the cease-fire. UNPROFOR was given a mandate of an 'interim nature' that included the following tasks:

1. To consolidate the cease-fire throughout the UNPAs;
2. To demilitarise the UNPAs;
3. To protect the local population against the threat or use of force;
4. To assist the displaced persons who wished to return to their homes.

The UN's peacekeeping mission in Croatia was clearly aimed at 'freezing' the situation on the ground at the time of the January 1992 cease-fire pending a final political settlement, rather as happened in Cyprus after the Turkish intervention there in 1974. However, even this limited mandate was not fulfilled by UNPROFOR except for the first item, and even then only in the sense that a new, full-scale Croat-Serb war was avoided.

By December 1991, an arbitration commission, set up with an eminent French constitutional lawyer and former President of the French Constitutional Court, Judge Robert Badinter, at its head, had reported back. Its main conclusion was that

Yugoslavia was in a 'state of dissolution'; that self-determination must not involve changes to existing republican borders at the time of independence (except where the parties concerned agreed otherwise); that the Serbs of Croatia and Bosnia were entitled to all the rights accorded to minorities under international law; and that Macedonia and Slovenia should be given diplomatic recognition. Bosnia could also be recognised if the majority of its population voted for independence at a referendum. The EU governments acted on Badinter's proposals, but by then the main role in handling the conflict in Yugoslavia had passed on to the UN.

Of course, as an organisation the EU faced formidable problems in dealing with the Yugoslav conflict. In the first place, it had no experience of dealing with such situations: trade and finance had been its proper *métier*. It lacked a permanent body for dealing with conflict resolution. Its presidency changed every six months. It did enjoy enormous prestige as a successful economic organisation and, therefore, possessed influence in the economic sphere. But that hardly mattered once the political conflict in Yugoslavia had escalated into a war. So what made the EU so eager to get involved in the Yugoslav crisis?

The United States had criticised the EU for its disunity and hesitancy during the Gulf war. The EU therefore wished to demonstrate that it was capable of a cohesive foreign policy in a region close to it geographically. The fact that the crisis was in Yugoslavia, a long-standing protégé of the EU, made it difficult to resist the temptation of telling the Americans that this particular 'spot of bother' could be dealt with by the Europeans alone. But the EU had convinced itself that all that was wanted was diplomatic mediation, overlooking the fundamental truth that no diplomatic effort could hope to succeed without leverage, including, ultimately, the threat of force. There was a reason for the EU's abandonment at the very start of the crisis of any serious consideration of the use of force. It was closely related to what had been happening in Eastern and Central Europe. The reluctance of Mikhail Gorbachev to use force to preserve the Soviet sphere of control there had fed the West European governments' illusion that everybody had come to share its belief in the effectiveness of peaceful multilateral diplomacy.

The attribution of Western values to those not sharing them had bedevilled the EU's (as well as, later, the UN's) attempts at peacemaking in South-Eastern Europe right from the beginning. Those concerned with the peace process had presumed that, sooner or later, given the right diplomatic framework, the 'warring factions' would sit down with each other and negotiate a settlement. However, this attitude ignored the fact that in the Yugoslav conflict the stronger (and apparently winning) side—the JNA and the Serbs—had absolutely no incentive to pull back in response to moral exhortations not backed by an explicit (or at least implied) threat of retaliatory action in case warnings against the use of force were ignored. On the contrary, Slobodan Milošević and the generals in Belgrade heard constantly from senior Western government figures that the use of force had been ruled out. Since Western governments had, in any case, no intention of intervening militarily, it could be argued that such statements were in fact accurately reflecting existing attitudes and that for Western politicians to do otherwise would have been an invitation to somebody to call their bluff. Even so, Western insistence that no force would be used provided Belgrade with an additional (and most welcome) source of reassurance that it had absolutely nothing to fear from the West.

Was there anything else the West could have done? Pessimists who dominated Western discussions at the time were probably right to argue that the locals, left to themselves, would have failed to agree either to a looser Yugoslavia or to its peaceful dissolution like that of the Swedish-Norwegian kingdom in 1905. This meant that they were probably likely to drift into war. However, the concerned West was not totally powerless to stop the tragedy, but it would have had to have an open-minded attitude: ruling out no solution—not even Yugoslavia's demise—instead of clinging far too long to an untenable *status quo*. Further, it would have had to demonstrate the political will to mediate a settlement and then attempt to enforce its implementation in an effective and credible way. As it was, neither of those pre-conditions was met. Instead of de-recognising Yugoslavia, as it should have done, the West stuck too long to the fiction—for that is what it was—that the conflict of Yugoslavia was a civil war within a sovereign state. As a consequence, Serbia and the JNA were able to present themselves as defenders of legality and constitutionality, with Croatia and Slovenia as law breaking 'secessionists'. By treating the JNA gently and respectfully as if it was a disinterested professional force standing above the political fray, and by offering diplomatic mediation on that basis, the Western governments gave Milošević and the JNA valuable time to extend and consolidate their conquests in Croatia.

Even worse was the imposition by the EU (and later also by the UN) of an arms embargo on the whole region of Yugoslavia. That handed a huge advantage to the stronger side in the war—the JNA and the Serbian paramilitaries—which had no need of foreign arms and ammunition imports, being able to rely on Yugoslavia's large arms industry, most of it situated in Serbia and Bosnia and Herzegovina. In Slovenia, the Serbian/JNA's advantage was to a certain extent offset by the Slovenes' success in keeping most of their territorial defence weapons, but the same was not true in Croatia or, later, in Bosnia and Herzegovina whose multi–ethnic territorial defence force was, like Croatia's, disarmed while Bosnian Serb supporters of Belgrade were handed the arms by the JNA.

Meanwhile the EU governments allowed themselves to become bogged down in the sterile and divisive debate about the diplomatic recognition of those Yugoslav republics that sought it. All in all, the EU took more than six months to recognise Croatia and Slovenia, another three months to recognise Bosnia and Herzegovina and another year and a half to do the same for Macedonia. Conventional wisdom in Britain, France and some other Western states continues to claim to this day that, even so, recognition of Croatia and Slovenia by the EU in January 1992, advocated by Germany and opposed by Britain and France in particular, had been 'premature'; that the Germans were wrong to press for it; and that it would have been wiser to wait for the resolution of all the outstanding problems (including that of the protection of the minorities) as Lord Carrington, Chairman of the 1991 Peace Conference on Yugoslavia, had demanded.

Was a 'Yugoslav' solution, for which Lord Carrington and most Western governments were clearly still hoping, at that stage still possible? Probably not, but the moot point is that, while the talking was going on at the Hague and in Brussels, the JNA and Serbian paramilitaries were continuing to wage war in Croatia and occupying ever more of its territory. Croatia could have been asked to wait for diplomatic recognition but only by those who were ready, pending such recognition, to protect it from the offensive by the JNA and the Serbian paramilitaries, then in full swing. For example, the WEU warships could easily have offered naval protection, patrolling the Adriatic at the time, to the city of Dubrovnik, which was being shelled by the besieging JNA forces made up of Montenegrin units in October and November 1991. The Western governments offered only diplomacy

The controversy over recognition will go on but it is now accepted even by those, like the Germans, who supported early diplomatic recognition, that it had only limited value. Recognition did serve notice on the JNA and Milošević that they could no longer reckon on international support for, or even acquiescence in, an attempt to put Yugoslavia together by force. But that did not bring the war in Croatia to an end. The war ended because the JNA and its allies, having occupied nearly a third of Croatia, had run out of steam and needed a breathing space to consolidate their gains and, meanwhile, prepare for the next stage of their campaign— against next-door Bosnia and Herzegovina. They calculated (quite correctly, as it turned out) that the stationing of UN troops in Croatia, which followed the cease-fire of January 1992 would help 'freeze'—to their advantage—the existing territorial situation, at least for the foreseeable future, as it had done in Cyprus in 1974.

The Serb minority issue, which figured prominently in the EU's discussions about Croatia's recognition (the issue did not arise in Slovenia because it had no sizeable ethnic minorities) was resolved by Germany, acting on behalf of the EU, persuading Zagreb to enlarge the scope of Serbian autonomy in the Croat Constitution. This was duly done, but the sincerity of the Croatian government was never put to the test because a significant part of Croatia's 600,000–strong Serb minority had, with encouragement from Belgrade and the JNA stationed in Croatia, taken up arms against the new Croatian government as early as the summer of 1990, without waiting to discuss the status and the rights of the Serbian minority. That rebellion made the future position of the Croatian Serbs more, not less, difficult because it convinced many Croats that it was they who needed protecting from an externally supported aggressive Serb minority, not the other way round.

In reality, tensions in the EU over the recognition issue had less to do with Croatia's suitability for recognition than with the mistrust towards reunited Germany felt by some EU members. Germany's pressure for the recognition of Croatia, was interpreted by them as a sign of its readiness to throw its weight about and a pointer to its future hegemonic ambitions in South-Eastern Europe. Actually, the focus of united Germany's economic, security and diplomatic interests was then—as it still is—not on South-Eastern Europe, but on Russia and the other successor states of the Soviet Union as well as on Central Europe. Germany's motive was principally humanitarian. The German government, including its Foreign Minister, Hans-Dietrich Genscher, had for years been very friendly with Belgrade but was in 1991 obliged to respond to the demands of German domestic opinion, partly influenced by the numerous Croatian 'guest-workers' there, for something to be done to stop the slaughter in Croatia. That was more fully reported by the German print and electronic media than those in other European countries and the United States. Besides, German politicians and officials alike were sympathetic to Croatia and Slovenia's demand for a right to self-determination because the same right that had recently been invoked as a justification for Germany's own reunification. The critics of the German position did have a point in one respect, at least. The logical follow-up to Croatia's diplomatic recognition could have been Croatia's request, as a sovereign state, for assistance against external aggression. Since Germany's 1949 Constitution severely limited the nation's scope for military action abroad, except strictly in self-defence, the burden of international response to demands for external help would have fallen not on its shoulders but on those of its allies. In other words, Germany was calling for others to be ready to do what it knew it could not reasonably be asked to do itself. The diplomatic recognition debate within the EU provided further confirmation of the proposition that, on this occasion too, the agenda being addressed by the EU had little or nothing to do with the situation on the ground and had everything to do with new intra-European relationships in the wake of Germany's unification.

Bosnia's tragic triangle

The Western governments' hesitant record over Croatia in 1991 made it more difficult for them to act constructively when Bosnia arrived on the agenda in early 1992. By its failure to act early and decisively to stop the war in Croatia, the West as a whole—including the United States—had lost in the region much of the credibility acquired during the Cold War and reinforced in the Gulf War. Many people in the region were deeply disappointed by the Western governments' failure to live up to their oft-repeated statements of support for the principle that the aggressor must be punished, but they never completely abandoned hope that Western politicians would ultimately be shamed into supporting the victims of aggression. That hope sustained its main victims, the Bosnian Moslems, throughout the course of the war. But the Serb/JNA leadership in Belgrade took the opposite view, which proved to be the correct one. Encouraged by the earlier displays of Western unwillingness to get involved, Belgrade concluded that it had nothing to fear, provided Western governments were from time to time handed convenient excuses for not intervening.

For a long time the course of the war in Bosnia provided ample backing for this view. Bosnia and Herzegovina was recognised as an independent state by the EU on 6 April 1992 and by the United States shortly thereafter. It became a member of the United Nations, together with Croatia and Slovenia, on 22 May. Bosnia's recognition was the last stage of a process devised at the end of 1991 with the aim of dealing with the legal implications of Yugoslavia's dissolution. The EU understood that Bosnia and Herzegovina had to seek independence because otherwise it would stay part of a rump Yugoslavia under Belgrade's control. Bosnia and Herzegovina was asked by the EU to hold a referendum on independence as a precondition for diplomatic recognition. The referendum, held on 29 February and 1 March 1992, was boycotted by most of Bosnia's Serbs at the urging of Radovan Karadžić, a Montenegrin by birth and an ally of Slobodan Milošević, who led the main Serbian party in Bosnia (SDS). Of the 64 per cent of Bosnia's registered voters who took part in the referendum, 93 per cent (in effect, the Croats and Moslems) voted in favour of independence. From the international community's point of view, the result was clear. The majority of Bosnians had voted for a democratic and independent Bosnia of equal citizens.

Milošević, Karadžić and JNA generals used the referendum as a pretext to start carving up Bosnia according to a long-term plan leading to the creation of a Greater Serbia, while a new Bosnian Croat leadership, installed under instructions from the government of President Tuđman in Zagreb, started working for a partition of Bosnia (see Chapter II). The international community responded in two ways: by diplomacy, and by providing the undoubtedly much-needed humanitarian aid under the protection of the UN (UNPROFOR), whose main task was the guarding of humanitarian convoys. But the lightly armed UN peacekeepers had no mandate to intervene to protect the population, let alone assist those who were resisting the Serb forces and the JNA. The embargo on arms imports into the region continued in force, obviously to the advantage of the well armed JNA and Serb forces. The UN added to it in May 1992 economic sanctions against the Federal Republic of Yugoslavia (FRY), which had been formed at the end of April by Serbia and Montenegro.

In mid-1992 the Western governments rejected a Turkish plan for a limited military intervention in Bosnia and strove to maintain strict neutrality towards the 'warring sides', as they used to be referred to officially. While the fighting (including the Serbian siege of Sarajevo) went on, the European Union and the UN continued the search for a peaceful solution. In July 1994 an international plan for Bosnia was put forward by the so-called 'Contact Group', made up of the UK, France, Germany, Russia and the United States (Italy joined in 1995). The Contact Group proposed that the Serb entity should be reduced to 49 per cent of the territory of Bosnia and Herzegovina, in other words that it should give up 20 per cent of the territory it was controlling. This plan was supported by Serbia, which urged the Bosnian Serbs to accept it. Milošević was anxious for a speedy end to the conflict in Bosnia. This was, first of all, because Serbia was in serious economic difficulties, and second, because Milošević considered that Serbian war aims had been achieved with the formation of Serb statelets in Bosnia and Croatia, which could in the fullness of time join Serbia. Besides, the new Federal Republic of Yugoslavia (FRY) could, as the legal successor of the old SFRY, expect that, if it cooperated with the West, sanctions would be lifted and Western financial assistance resumed. The leaders of the Bosnian Serbs rejected the plan and this led in August 1994 to a breaking off by Belgrade of political and economic relations with the RS and the imposition of a blockade.

The isolated and embittered RS regime embarked on ever more aggressive policies. These included the shelling on 25 May 1995 of Tuzla, killing seventy-one civilians; the capture on 11 July 1995 of the UN-protected Srebrenica and Žepa where an estimated 8,000 Bosniak men were massacred; and on 28 August 1995 the shelling of the Markale a market in Sarajevo, in which forty-one civilians were killed The RS regime responded to the threat of a NATO bombing by the capture of 370 UN soldiers as hostages, who were deliberately placed close to the likely targets of NATO bombing. From 30 August to 13 September, NATO carried out air strikes against military targets and infrastructure in the RS which weakened still further the morale of its already demoralised forces. In a joint Croat-Bosniak offensive, in which Croatia's regular army also participated, 23 per cent of the RS territory was captured. The war in Bosnia and Herzegovina ended with the conclusion of the peace agreement in Dayton, Ohio, on 21 November 1995 and its signing in Paris on 14 December.

This, however, did not mean the end of the war in the whole of former Yugoslavia. As already described in the previous chapter, Kosovo, neglected for years by the world community, came on the agenda in 1997 when ethnic Albanian frustration over Belgrade's failure to relax its repressive policy in the province introduced in 1989 found its expressions in a guerrilla campaign waged by a body calling itself the Kosovo Liberation Army (UÇK). Western governments, which had in 1993–1995 come to regard Milošević as a partner in the search for peace in Croatia and Bosnia, urged him to relax his tight grip on Kosovo, but he refused and indeed stepped up efforts to crush the insurgency by savage reprisals in Kosovo. This attempt misfired. As described earlier, a NATO bombing campaign against Serbia started on 24 March 1999 and ended after two-and-a-half months with the withdrawal of the Serbian forces and the administration from Kosovo and the near-complete return of the 800,000 or so ethnic Albanians who were expelled, or had fled, from Kosovo into the neighbouring states before and during the NATO bombing campaign.

In contrast to their hesitant attitude during the war in Croatia in 1991 and much of the subsequent war in Bosnia, Western governments quite early on in the Kosovo crisis identified Serbia as the chief culprit and resolved to defeat it—though stopping short of accompanying their bombing campaign with a land war and carrying it into Serbia proper. Kosovo was placed under a temporary UN administration. After nearly a decade of war, the time had come to start building the peace.

Towards reconstruction and reconciliation

Unlike Central Europe and the Baltic region, where all the states are members both of the European Union and of NATO, a number of South-Eastern European states are (as of end-2009) outside both. At the beginning of 2008, three of the states—Bulgaria, Romania and Slovenia—were in NATO and the same three in the European Union. The process, which the locals like to call 'Euro-Atlantic integration', is proceeding slowly. It began after the end of the military conflict in Bosnia and Herzegovina and the signing of the Dayton Agreement. It was then that a number of regional initiatives, championed by the European Union, the United States, NATO and the international financial institutions such as the World Bank (WB), the European Bank for Reconstruction and Development (EBRD) and the European Investment Bank (EIB) were launched. All were aimed at strengthening political and economic stability in the region. They had to be initiated from outside South-Eastern Europe, because the locals for a variety of reasons share few clearly perceived common interests. Unfortunately, some of those outside initiatives, though well intentioned, were poorly defined, coordinated and funded, with correspondingly little impact on the ground.

The first such post-Dayton initiative was the Royaumont Process for Stability and Good Neighbourliness in South-East

Europe, launched in 1996 by France and later on adopted by the EU. It brought together Albania, Bosnia and Herzegovina, Bulgaria, Croatia, FR Yugoslavia (as it then was), Hungary, Macedonia, Romania, Slovenia and Turkey, the EU-15, the United States, the Russian Federation, the Council of Europe and the Organisation for Security and Cooperation in Europe (OSCE). The aim of the process was to prepare, select and finance projects likely to help stability and ensure good neighbourliness in the region. It also involved strengthening inter-parliamentary activities and organising seminars, conferences and NGO meetings.

The US-sponsored Southeast European Cooperation Initiative (SECI), also launched in 1996, aimed at supporting the implementation of the Dayton Agreement It concentrated on mostly privately funded economic cooperation and reconstruction of the region in the fields of infrastructure, trade, transport, energy, the environment and private sector development. Its pragmatic, quite well focused approach has yielded results in cross-border cooperation and the fight against trans-border crime.

The South-East European Cooperation Process (SEECP), a locally originated forum launched in 2000, took in Albania, Bosnia and Herzegovina, Bulgaria, Croatia, Greece, Macedonia. Moldova, Montenegro, Romania, Serbia and Turkey. It concentrated, with little to show for it, on political cooperation and dialogue, covering issues such as security, economic cooperation, humanitarian, social and cultural cooperation as well as cooperation in the fields of justice and home affairs. This body has for some time been in serious need of rethinking its rationale.

The Stability Pact for South-Eastern Europe (SP) was launched by Germany, with the support of the European Union and under the auspices of the OSCE, in June 1999 in the immediate aftermath of the Kosovo conflict. The aims were: to help overcome the instability and local conflicts in the Balkans; to foster regional cooperation; and to support the region's integration with the rest of Europe and the Atlantic region. It was set up as a vehicle for intergovernmental cooperation among twenty-eight states and a number of international organisations. Albania, Bosnia and Herzegovina, Bulgaria, Croatia, Moldova, Macedonia, Romania, and Serbia and Montenegro (initially as the FRY) were participants from the region (all except Moldova and the FRY were involved from the start). The principal body was the Regional Table including all the SP governments and international organisations and chaired by a Special Coordinator. In addition, three Working Tables were established: on democratisation and human rights; on economic reconstruction, development and cooperation; and on security issues. In Working Table II, the EU assumed a leading role over trade facilitation and liberalisation, infrastructure, energy and social cohesion while sharing with the World Bank the responsibility for coordinating economic aid to the region. The EBRD led a number of private sector initiatives designed to foster investment and entrepreneurship in the region.

The Stability Pact was seen at first on the ground in the region as a channel for injecting huge international aid into it, even a sort of a latter-day Marshall Plan for South-Eastern Europe. In practice, it turned out to be no more than a moderately useful instrument for coordinating a range of existing international efforts. After the appointment of Erhard Busek, former Austrian Vice-Chancellor, as Coordinator in 2002, the SP was slimmed down and streamlined and became more closely associated with the EU's policy in the region. In 2006 a Regional Cooperation Coucil (RCC) was set up to guide the SP towards becoming a regionally-owned structure, a sort of South-East European counterpart to the Northern Dimension. The RCC has its headquarters in Sarajevo, and the first meeting took place in February 2008. The SP was closed down on 30 June 2008.

EU expansion and integration

The European Union has been, and still is, the most serious and important international player in the region both in economic and political terms, not least as the main driving force towards economic and political reform in South-Eastern Europe. A different approach has been adopted towards Bulgaria, Romania and Slovenia on the one hand and the so-called Western Balkans group of states (Albania and the states of former Yugoslavia minus Slovenia) on the other. Regional cooperation was for the Western Balkans group a prerequisite for integration, while in the case of Central and East European countries cooperation was only encouraged.

Slovenia, which was only lightly brushed by the war that engulfed Croatia, Bosnia and later Kosovo, relatively easily met the criteria for EU membership and began the negotiations for EU accession in 1998. At a referendum in March 2003, 89.61 per cent of voters approved the idea of joining the EU. Slovenia's accession to the EU took place on 1 May 2004 together with the rest of the Central Europe and Baltic group of states. On 1 January 2007 Slovenia became the first country among the new intake in 2004 to adopt the euro.

Romania, still a Communist country in 1974 was in that year included in the then EC's Generalised System of Preferences. In 1980 an agreement on industrial production was signed with the EC. Romania established diplomatic relations with the EC in 1990 and signed with it in 1991 an agreement on trade and cooperation. In 1995 it signed a Europe Agreement with the EU and in the same year applied for EU membership, but membership negotiations started only in 2000. The European Council of December 2002 set 2007 as the date for Romania's accession. In 2004 the European Commission set a safety clause for Romania (and Bulgaria), which stipulated that accession could be delayed by one year by a unanimous decision of the European Council if the country failed to meet the targets. In April 2005 Romania signed the EU Accession Treaty at the same time as Bulgaria. The European Parliament backed Romania's prospective accession with 497 votes to ninety-three and seventy-one abstentions In September 2006, the European Union gave the green light for Romania's accession but insisted on further reforms. If those were not met, Brussels could invoke safeguards including the suspension of EU grounds. On 1 January 2007 Romania joined the EU, but temporary restrictions on movement of labour to other EU countries were imposed both on Romania and Bulgaria.

Bulgaria signed an agreement on association with the EU in 1993, which came into force in 1995. It applied for EU membership in December 1995. Preliminary membership negotiations started in 1997 and full negotiations opened in February 2000 and were concluded in June 2004. Bulgaria signed the Treaty of Accession with the EU on 25 April 2005, which was ratified by the Bulgarian parliament the following month. In September 2006 the European Commission published its last monitoring report on Bulgaria's progress towards membership, which noted continuing concerns over certain issues including organised crime, which would continue to be monitored from Brussels for a limited period. Bulgaria joined the EU on 1 January 2007.

For the Western Balkans group of states, the EU-decreed Regional Approach meant in practice that trade preferences, financial assistance and the establishment of contractual relations were subject to different degrees of conditionality, but that the readiness of each country to engage in cross-border cooperation was to be monitored at all stages of the development of relations. Cooperation was, in other words, made compulsory while conditionality was applied on a case-by-case basis. The failure of the FRY, Croatia and Bosnia and Herzegovina to meet the condition of satisfactory compliance with the International Criminal Tribunal for the Former Yugoslavia (ICTY) caused them to lag behind, for example. None of the countries concerned liked the EU's regional approach, chiefly because they feared that their progress towards EU membership would be delayed by the laggards in the group, whoever they might be at a particular moment. The regional approach in fact became a source of tension and division in the region.

In May 1999 the European Commission adopted a new approach, the Stabilisation and Association Process (SAP), aimed at helping the region towards political and economic stabilisation while also developing a closer association with the EU. The SAP gave three promises. The first was that of economic and financial assistance through the Phare and Obnova programmes and then, after 2001, through the CARDS programme as well as through financial aid and balance of payments support. The second was to liberalise trade between the EU and the SAP countries. The third was that of eventual EU memberships via the Stabilisation and Association Agreements (SAAs), to be concluded once the EU's conditionality had been met. The SAA was regarded as the first step in the EU accession process to be followed by candidacy and then by the opening of negotiations for full membership.

Important political changes—the election of a centre-left, strongly European-minded government in Croatia in January 2000 and, in October 2000, the fall of the Milošević regime in Serbia and the formation of a broadly-based democratic coalition (see Chapter III)—accelerated the EU accession process in the region. At the summit in Zagreb in November 2000, the Western Balkan groups of countries agreed to a clear set of conditions and objectives in return for the EU's offers of the prospect of accession and assistance programmes to support that aim. Regional cooperation was an important part of that deal. In April 2001 Macedonia signed the SAA with the EU and was followed by Croatia in October 2001. For the FRY the opening of SAA negotiations was made conditional on the renegotiation of the relationship between Serbia and Montenegro as constituent parts of the federation. Albania was close to negotiating an SAA, while Bosnia and Herzegovina was not yet considered ready.

The EU-Western Balkans Summit in Thessaloniki in June 2003 reinforced the European perspectives of the Western Balkans and enlarged the SAPs with new instruments modelled on those negotiated previously with Central and East European states. The summit stressed that the pace of the process of accession would depend on each country's performance in implementing reforms and respecting the SAP conditionality, as well as respect for the so-called Copenhagen political criteria set by the 1993 European Council. These criteria require a country to be a stable democracy, to have a working market economy, and to adopt the common rules, standards and policies that make up the body of EU law (*acquis communautaire*). The EU continued to strive, with varying success, to strike a balance between the regional approach and bilateralism.

In June 2004 Croatia became the first member of the Western Balkans group to get the status of a candidate for EU membership. Since then, all the states of the region have made some progress:

Albania signed its SAA in June 2006 but further progress in accession negotiations depends on the reform of the electoral system and other reforms in the run-up to the general election in 2009. It applied for EU membership in April 2009.

Bosnia and Herzegovina initialled its SAA in December 2007 and signed it on 16 June 2008 against the background of a political situation, disturbed by the fallout from Kosovo's declaration of independence, which has led to renewed public demands in Bosnia's Serb entity for a referendum on the entity's independence. Bosnia and Herzegovina still remains, as it has been since the signing of the Dayton Agreements in 1995, a *de facto* protectorate, under the overall supervision of the High Representative, appointed by the international community, who is also EU Special Representative. Ever since 1997 his powers have included the right to impose legislation, remove political officials and veto public appointments His main task in recent years has been to guide the reforming process as part of the country's preparation for eventual membership of the European Union

Croatia opened accession negotiations with the EU in June 2006, but those stalled in the run-up to the general election in November 2007. By February 2008 only sixteen chapters of the *acquis* had been opened and two provisionally closed. As negotiations were about to resume, a dispute arose between Croatia on the one side and Italy and Slovenia on the other over the introduction by Croatia on 1 January 2008 of an environmental and fisheries protection zone in the Adriatic. To prevent the dispute derailing Croatia's EU accession negotiations, an urgent search for a compromise was initiated. Such a compromise was found. However, the prospect that Croatia could be the first country in the Western Balkans group to complete its accession negotiations and join the EU in 2011 was threatened by a territorial dispute with Slovenia. In 2008 and 2009 Slovenia slowed down the accession process by deciding to block a number of *acquis* chapters, pending prior agreement with Croatia on the settlement of outstanding territorial issues.

Macedonia received in 2001 much active diplomatic help from the European Union, acting in cooperation with the United States, when the country faced the danger of civil war involving the ethnic Albanian guerrillas and the government in Skopje. Western governments' representatives helped achieve a cease-fire as well as the signing in August of that year of the so-called Ohrid Agreement on constitutional reform. The country achieved official candidate-for-membership status in December 2005, but the actual negotiations have not yet started. In February 2008 the European Commission defined eight key reform areas that needed to be tackled before further progress can be made. There is also a threat of an indefinite delay coming from another quarter: Greece's insistence on the prior resolution of its dispute with Macedonia over its official name.

Montenegro signed its SAA in October 2007 and applied for EU membership in April 2009. Serbia initialled the SAA in November 2007 but the actual signing and granting of its candidacy status was made conditional on full cooperation with the ICTY. The deterioration of relations between Serbia and the EU over the decision by the EU in February 2008 to recognise Kosovo's independence (though leaving the timing to individual member states) introduced a new barrier to Serbia's progress towards EU accession. The SAA was signed in April 2008, and Serbia's improved cooperation with ICTY following the arrest and extradition to The Hague of Rado-van Karadžić in July 2008 has improved Serbia's EU pros-pects. A major step forward for Kosovo was the decision by the IMF in May 2009 to receive it into membership, followed by the invitation in June to join the World Bank. Kosovo is included in the Stabilisation and Association Pro-cess through the SAP Tracking Mechanism, established in Nov-ember 2002 as a forum for dialogue between Kosovo and the EU within the framework of the UN Security Council Resolu-tion 1244 of June 1999. At the international donor conference on Kosovo in July 2008 all twenty-seven EU member-states supported the initiative to provide Kosovo with €1.2 billion in the 2008–2011 period, with the EU pledging €508 million.

Ever since the European Union turned its full attention towards South-Eastern Europe in the mid-1990s following the end of the war in Bosnia, it has played a hugely important role as the main driver of political and economic reform and regional cooperation in the whole area. The rejection of the draft EU Constitutional Treaty at referendums in France and the Netherlands in 2005 was widely interpreted as an indica-tion of growing 'enlargement fatigue', aggravated by total opposition in several EU countries to Turkey's eventual acces-sion as a full member. In the meantime, a new reform treaty was signed by all twenty-seven EU member countries in Lis-bon in December 2007, thus removing various procedural obstacles to further enlargement (provided the treaty is rati-fied by all countries). Also, as has often happened in the past, the threat that the dispute over Serbia's opposition to Kos-ovo's independence could escalate into a full-blown crisis, threatening once again the peace and stability of the whole region of South-Eastern Europe, has forced the EU to give more urgency to its accession strategy for Western Balkans. In December 2007 the European Council affirmed its com-mitment, reiterated in February 2008, to full and effective support for the European perspective of the Western Balkans.

A sign of this new EU focus on the Western Balkans was the new initiative by the European Commission in March

2008. In a clear attempt to revive the optimistic and forward-looking spirit of the 2003 Thessaloniki programme for the region's progress towards the EU, the initiative calls for the mobilisation of all available instruments to support the region's progress towards EU membership. It also includes some concrete new proposals such as that for an urgent new dialogue aimed at establishing conditions for the lifting of visa requirements and for more scholarships for students from the Western Balkans to study in the EU. The initiative also called for discussions on a new, somewhat nebulous-looking scheme for a Transport Community Treaty for the Western Balkans.

The changing influence of the US and Russia

The role of the United States as a major player in the region was somewhat reduced in the early 1990s when policy-makers in Washington were much preoccupied with the Middle East and various other global challenges and were glad to leave the chief responsibility for South-Eastern Europe to its European allies. However, the US, pursuing its geo-strategic aims, continued to exercise decisive influence in crucial moments such as the end of the war in Bosnia in 1995, the bombing campaign against Serbia in 1999, and finally over the recognition of Kosovo in 2008. In the pursuit of its aims, the US uses NATO as its chief instrument. In April 2008 NATO invited Albania and Croatia to join, and would also have invited Macedonia if that country's membership had not been blocked by Greece because of the unresolved dispute over the country's name.

Russia, which emerged both militarily and economically seriously weakened from the collapse of the Soviet Union in 1992, was content during the Yeltsin years to play a relatively minor and on the whole cooperative role in the affairs of South-Eastern Europe. This changed under the presidency of Vladimir Putin, whose hallmark has been the reassertion of Russian influence everywhere, including in South-Eastern

Europe, chiefly by exercising its new position as an energy superpower. This had led to a new rivalry in Europe between Russia and the United States, which is likely to continue and even intensify. It is unlikely that the United States will be prepared to yield its dominant strategic position in South-Eastern Europe to Russia. Also, the increasing Russian assertiveness is likely to lead to a closing of Western ranks in South-Eastern Europe as indeed elsewhere. This will probably not stop Russia from trying to exploit its current influence in Serbia in order to re-establish a strong position in the region, resembling that enjoyed by the Soviet Union until the end of the Cold War. Such an attempt may cause some problems for the United States and the European Union in the region, but is unlikely seriously to challenge Western dominance there. The eventual absorption through the enlargement process—though at different speeds—of the Western Balkans in the EU is now on the cards. It is no exaggeration to say that this opens, quite literally, the best prospect the region has had in centuries.

5

ECONOMIC RECOVERY AND REFORMS

An economy rising from the ashes

The political upheavals in South-Eastern Europe over the past two decades, and the international community's response, have had a profound effect on economic developments in the region. The main events described in chapters II and III—especially the break-up of former Yugoslavia—still shape economic performance and living standards today. The previous chapter argued that the role of the international community has been broadly constructive in recent years, but there is a limit to what it can do to help the region recover in economic terms. Nevertheless, between 2000 and 2008 there was a broad-based and sustained economic recovery across the region. It may have come later than in Central Europe and the Baltic States but a catching-up process took place. This is the encouraging story that is often overlooked by commentators who focus on the problems rather than the long-term opportunities.

The reasons for the strong economic growth are varied. Businesses throughout the region showed resilience, adaptability to new circumstances, and a strong entrepreneurial spirit. Governments and other state authorities generally accepted the need for a thorough reform agenda and, to varying degrees, have pushed through and begun to implement difficult reforms. The positive effects of these reforms included rising living standards, record investment flows and increased opportunities for entrepreneurship. International institutions such as the EBRD and the World Bank provided both hard cash and valuable policy advice to help develop infrastructure and institutions and to promote a more conducive climate for private sector development. By the start of 2009, the region was no longer a stagnant backwater of Europe. While political issues still hang over it to some extent, the combination of progress in reforms and high GDP growth rates had transformed South-Eastern Europe into one of the most dynamic emerging market regions.

Many people, both inside the region and outside, fail to see things in this positive light. The sharp drop in economic activity in the first half of 2009 has given fuel to the pessimistic view. Even before the global crisis began to affect the region, recent survey evidence (discussed below) had suggested that people in South-Eastern Europe are generally quite gloomy about economic performance relative to other transition regions. Nostalgia for the past seems to be more prevalent here than in other former communist regions. Outside the region, there is still an image problem—for many potential foreign investors, the mention of the word 'Balkans' conjures up troubled images of war and conflict, rather than investment opportunities and economic potential. The path of transition has been a particularly uneven one in this part of the world, and the effects on people's lives seem to have been even more traumatic than in other parts of the former communist bloc. But there is little sign that this will put a 'brake' on further reform. Even though governments are (as of end-2009) preoccupied with grappling with the effects of the economic crisis, there are still signs of a desire to make further progress in institutional development.

ECONOMIC RECOVERY AND REFORMS

Background: preparing for transition

At the start of the 1990s, countries in South-Eastern Europe were, for different reasons, unprepared for the demands of transition. For a start, economic development had traditionally lagged behind the rest of Europe. Geography has always been a major part of the reason for this; the region was for a long time relatively remote from major western markets, while the relatively inhospitable terrain in parts of the region impeded trade and deterred foreign investors. But a more fundamental reason for the region's lack of preparedness was that countries were either distracted by the fall-out from the break-up of Yugoslavia, or were inheriting a system so dysfunctional that a total overhaul of all major public institutions would be needed before things could be put on the right track.

At the end of the 1980s, the strongest economy in the region was in Yugoslavia. Throughout the 1970s and most of the 1980s, most Yugoslavs enjoyed a standard of living that was the envy of those in the Soviet bloc. The country had by far the most advanced private sector in the region. In principle, this should have given the country an important head start in the transition. It is often said today that, had the country not been broken up, Yugoslavia would have been amongst the first, if not *the* first, of former socialist countries in Eastern Europe to join the European Union. But the Yugoslav social ownership model had severe weaknesses, namely the lack of a clear ownership structure and consequent inability to attract fresh capital and know-how. To a great extent, the economy was propped up by a mixture of three factors: state subsidies, foreign borrowing and remittances from Yugoslavs working abroad. Once foreign support began to dry up, and debts became due, it became progressively harder to keep the economy on track. The political convulsions the country was suffering from distracted attention from economic reforms and eventually pushed them off the agenda for years.

The starting circumstances for Bulgaria, Romania and Albania were even less propitious for a fast and successful transition. Bulgaria had been an orthodox, well-behaved member of the Soviet bloc, adhering rather rigidly to communist principles and generally showing a lack of economic dynamism and little tolerance for the idea of market forces. Romania under the Ceauşescu dictatorship had pursued a more idiosyncratic route, distancing itself from Moscow and hence attracting the occasional courtship from the West (see Chapter II) but increasingly pursuing an autarchic economic policy, with disastrous results. Worst of all was Albania, which took autarchy and Stalinist principles to the most extreme levels. Virtually all forms of private ownership or business were forbidden, investment from abroad was banned and foreign trade was extremely limited. Unlike other countries, Albania had no economic patrons once the break with China took place in 1978, and, as a result, it entered the new era as the poorest country in the region and with by far the most difficult starting point for transition.

Prior to the 1990s the degree of economic integration in the region was varied. The former Yugoslavia was one economic space, with strong trade and investment linkages among the six republics. This helps to explain why the subsequent economic decline in the newly established states was so severe, as these links were broken during the violent break-up of the SFRY. But in general, bilateral trade flows in south-eastern Europe were limited, while cross-border investment was virtually unknown. In 1989, the idea of South-Eastern Europe as an economic area where countries would engage in regional cooperation would have seemed totally far-fetched, had anyone proposed such an idea at the time.

Economic transition: the early years

Estimates of GDP at the start of the 1990s are subject to a large degree of uncertainty. The concept of GDP was not widely used or understood at the time in these countries; other concepts such as 'gross social product' were more in favour. But whatever the true measure of economic activity, it is clear that there was wide variation both within the former

Yugoslavia, and between Yugoslavia and other countries. For example, according to one set of estimates, GDP per capita in Slovenia in 1990 was US$8,706, and in Croatia it was US$5,106, compared to US$2,396 in Bosnia and Herzegovina. Elsewhere, both Bulgaria and Romania had a GDP per capita in 1990 of around US$1,300, while in Albania it was a mere US$ 638. Although 1990 was something of a high point compared to the deep recessions that followed, in fact the region had been struggling economically during the 1980s. In Yugoslavia, the problem of foreign debt management was becoming insuperable, creating concern among the international financial community (particularly among creditors) of a possible debt crisis.

The first half of the 1990s was disastrous for the region's economic development. Between 1990 and 1995, real GDP fell precipitously in most countries. Such an outcome was unprecedented and few were prepared for it. In retrospect, some reduction of output should have been expected. We now know that for any country serious about making the transition from state control to a market economy, an initial economic decline is virtually impossible to avoid. At the start of transition, however, many observers (in western academic circles at least) failed to predict the size of the recession that most countries suffered. Once the scale of collapse was apparent, various theories were put forward to explain why output fell so much, and arguments ensued about whether countries should pursue a 'shock therapy' approach to economic reform, or whether a more gradualist path would be better. For most countries throughout Central Europe and the Commonwealth of Independent States, this kind of academic debate was an irrelevant distraction; economic policy in the early years became an exercise in damage limitation. What made South-Eastern Europe different, however, is that the problems were compounded by a combination of particularly weak initial conditions and the political explosion at the heart of the region.

By far the worst case of economic collapse in the region was Bosnia and Herzegovina. The war from 1992 to 1995 had a catastrophic effect on the economy. Formal economic activity fell by anything up to 80 per cent of pre-war levels, although this is pure guesswork since no reliable statistics were gathered during this period. Bare survival was the goal for most people. During the Tito years, Bosnia and Herzegovina had been a centre of military production and heavy industry, but the war put paid to most of that, meaning that the economy had to start virtually from scratch once the war had ended.

Other former Yugoslav countries that fared especially badly in this period include the FRY and Macedonia. Wide-ranging UN sanctions were imposed on the FRY in spring 1992 and contributed to a severe economic decline that continued up to the point when the sanctions were partly reversed in 1996. More importantly, however, the sanctions led to a widespread criminalisation of the economy. Smuggling and other illegal activities became the norm, and formal economic activities suffered accordingly, since it became virtually impossible to carry out a business both profitably and in full compliance with the law. Meanwhile, Macedonia was suffering not only from the indirect effects of the sanctions on FRY, but also from an embargo imposed by the Greek government because of the dispute over the country's name. The economy had already collapsed in 1992 (real GDP fell by more than 20 per cent) and continued to decline between 1993 and 1995, at which point (in September) the embargo was lifted and a modest recovery began.

In contrast, Slovenia and Croatia managed to turn their economies around fairly quickly. Slovenia's economy began to grow in 1993 and has continued to do so until 2009. The Slovenian model is often cited as one that others should follow, since the transition recession was relatively short and the country achieved an enviable level of macroeconomic stability (cemented by its entry into the 'Eurozone' in January 2007) and prosperity. But such a view ignores the crucial role played by two factors—peace and geography. The success of Slovenia in escaping from Yugoslavia relatively painlessly (see Chapter II) and its favourable location adjacent to prosperous EU countries (Austria and Italy) have undoubtedly helped the Slovenian economy become by some distance the richest (in per capita terms) in the region—nearly US$23,000 in 2007. Croatia also benefited from achieving relatively quickly a ceasefire in hostilities, and a strong stabilisation programme instituted in 1994 helped build a robust recovery.

During the early 1990s Bulgaria and Romania suffered classical transition recessions. Three factors contributed to the severity of the recession in both countries. First, both relied to a greater extent than central European transition countries on trade with the former Soviet Union. When this collapsed, the resulting downturn was correspondingly severe. Second, any progress in liberalisation prior to 1990 had been extremely hesitant or non-existent, in contrast to some central European countries such as Hungary, for example, where some market-oriented reforms were introduced in the 1980s. And third, both countries were slow to implement serious efforts at stabilisation, meaning that when recovery came, it was fragile and did not last long (see below for more discussion).

During the first half of the decade, the economy with some of the highest levels of annual growth in South-Eastern Europe was Albania. Many people were surprised at the time, but should not have been once it was recognised where Albania was starting from. Not only did it enter the 1990s with a totally outdated and dysfunctional economy, but the early period of transition (1991–92) was marked by widespread economic destruction, looting and general mayhem as the population's pent-up frustrations erupted. Seen in this context, the high growth rates that followed were only to be expected. The economy was also boosted in this period by a massive inflow of remittances, a new phenomenon for the Albanian economy because emigration prior to 1991 was virtually impossible. Like Bulgaria and Romania however, but to a much more severe extent, the early recovery in Albania proved to be built on weak foundations, as shown in more detail in the next section.

IN SEARCH OF THE BALKAN RECOVERY

The second half of the 1990s: recovery and reversals

The year 1996 appeared to mark a turning point for the region's economies. The end of the war in Bosnia and Herzegovina in late-1995 helped to create a sense of a new beginning for the region. The anti–Milošević protests (see Chapter III) in major Serbian cities in winter 1996/1997 reflected the impatience of Serbian people to move on from the past and push ahead with reforms, both political and economic. By this time too, Slovenia had received clear signals that it would be among the frontrunners for EU membership, Croatia was recovering well after a firm stabilisation programme had taken root and Macedonia was also stabilising, following the removal of the Greek embargo in September 2005. Elsewhere, the Bulgarian and Romanian economies were growing rapidly while Albania was booming, with real GDP growth in 1995 of more than 13 per cent.

The path of economic progress at the time seemed to be consistent with an emerging 'stylised fact' of transition countries, namely, the 'U-shaped' path of economic performance. This means that after an initial drop in output, most countries in transition started to recover and saw output rise again. The second half of the 1990s was generally a period of recovery across the whole transition region, although there were some exceptions. By that stage, most countries had put in place a macroeconomic stabilisation programme and had begun a comprehensive set of transition reforms. An academic literature began to emerge at the time, showing that a combination of three broad factors—structural reforms, lower inflation and fiscal deficits, and favourable initial conditions—underpinned the recovery and growth that transition countries started to enjoy.

In the case of South-Eastern Europe, however, the situation in the second half of the decade was more complicated than, for example, in Central Europe or the Baltic states. Several countries suffered reversals which brought their temporary recoveries to a halt. The Kosovo conflict in 1999, which affected not only the FRY but also had important spillover economic effects on the whole region, was another major blow to the recovery process. Rather than a conventional U-shape, therefore, the path of GDP in many countries resembled more a 'W-shape'—recovery, followed by reversal and then recovery again. A series of economic crises hit the region prior to the Kosovo conflict, first in Bulgaria, and then in Romania and Albania.

The Bulgarian economic crisis in 1996–97 was a major setback for the country. Real GDP fell by 9.4 per cent in 1996 and by a further 5.6 per cent in 1997, while the annual rate of inflation at one point rose to more than 1000 per cent. The problem lay in the failure of the authorities to implement serious reforms, especially in the financial sector. For years the banking system had been used by the government to prop up the unreformed state enterprise sector, leading to large and hidden losses in the banking sector. This led to an acceleration in inflation and when the banks eventually tried to tighten liquidity in 1995, people lost confidence in them, leading to a number of banking failures and a sharp drop in economic activity.

In common with Bulgaria, Romania maintained a system of subsidies for enterprises for a long time, as well as tolerating bad loans in the banking system. The problems were effectively concealed for some time as the economy grew in 1994–96, helped by a major expansion in domestic demand. But these policies were accompanied by increasing exposure to external financing. The global financial crisis of 1997 meant that this source of money tightened and the government had no option but to try to stabilise the economy. The result was a drop in inflation but also a deep recession that was not reversed until the year 2000, and only slowly thereafter for a couple of years.

The most spectacular collapse during this time was in Albania in 1997. At the time, the banking sector was still mostly state-owned and in very poor shape, and confidence in banks among the population was low. Nevertheless, incomes were growing sharply, helped by the expanding economy and large remittance flows from Albanians working abroad. Many people began to have, for the first time in their lives, some savings but did not know what to do with them. In the absence of a properly functioning private banking sector, these savings were increasingly channelled into questionable schemes that offered suspiciously high interest rates, sometimes of the order of 5–6 per cent per month. One of the largest schemes appeared to have the implicit backing of the state, leading people to believe that their savings would be secure. Of course all of these funds were essentially pyramid schemes, and their inevitable collapse in early 1997 led to widespread anarchy and the fall of the then government. However, the economy recovered more quickly than many expected. Once basic security was restored, things rapidly returned to normal and GDP in 1998 was similar (in real terms) to the level recorded in 1996.

In the former Yugoslav republics, the period from 1996–99 saw significant growth in most cases, but the reasons differed significantly from one country to the next. For several years, the highest growth rates, not surprisingly, were in Bosnia and Herzegovina, as the post-war period saw massive inflows of foreign aid and donor-supported investment. Croatia too saw a significant rebound while the Slovenian economy continued to expand nicely, with steady annual growth rates averaging between 4 and 5 per cent. But elsewhere, the picture was less encouraging. Although the Greek embargo on Macedonia ended in 1995, the economy was slow to take off. The Macedonian authorities tried to boost exports by devaluing the currency in July 1997 by 16 per cent, but although any possible inflationary effects were contained by a public sector wage freeze, the devaluation did little to inject dynamism into the economy.

The FRY economy started to grow strongly during this time but, in an environment where the 'outer wall' of sanctions was still in place, corruption and illegality remained endemic and no serious reforms were implemented. The Milošević regime was able to buy some time by selling in late-

1996 49 per cent of the state-owned telecommunications company to Italian and Greek investors for approximately US$700 million and using part of the proceeds to pay wages and pensions. But the lack of reform and new investment prevented the economy from achieving anything close to its potential, and the country was still in a very difficult position when the Kosovo conflict erupted.

The Kosovo war—economic implications

The Kosovo conflict, and in particular the seventy-eight days of NATO air strikes between late-March and early-June 1999, not only had devastating human consequences, but was also a major setback to economic development in the region. The country most affected by far was the FRY, and Serbia in particular, but the conflict had an adverse impact throughout the region. Nevertheless, in some cases the economic consequences were less than initially feared, and Albania and Macedonia—the two main recipients of refugees during the crisis—showed surprising resilience.

The Serbian economy is estimated to have shrunk by about 18 per cent in 1999, as a result of the destruction of industrial facilities, the disruption to supply and trading routes and the lack of serious investment, either from domestic or foreign sources. The direct cost of the damage to infrastructure, including industrial facilities, was estimated at the time to be about US$3–4 billion. The government tried to maintain spending by printing more money, thereby boosting inflation, which was already running at an annual level of around 40 per cent, to even higher levels. At the time, economic prospects for Serbia appeared bleak because the end of the NATO air strikes in June-1999 was not accompanied by any change in government policy or any relaxation of international sanctions against the Milosevic regime. The situation at the time looked a little more promising in Montenegro, which had begun to focus on economic reforms and attracting interest from foreign investors, but the political atmosphere there was tense as the republic was still yoked together with Serbia.

Elsewhere in the region, the conflict adversely affected trade, investment, transportation and, in the case of Croatia, tourism. However, the costs in some cases were more limited than originally expected. Regarding trade for example, there were dire warnings initially of the impact the conflict would have on the Macedonian economy, since prior to the war about 20 per cent of its exports went directly to the FRY and the country relied on routes through Serbia to reach other markets. However, once the conflict had ended, a significant portion of this trade was re-directed to Kosovo to meet the huge, construction-related increase in demand from the province. As a result, the Macedonian economy grew by more than 4 per cent in 1999, significantly higher than in any previous year since independence. Albania, which absorbed the majority of the refugees from Kosovo, managed to grow by about 7 per cent in 1999, the same rate predicted by most observers even before the conflict began.

Encouragingly for long-term growth, foreign investors were relatively undeterred by the crisis, at least in the larger economies. Between them, Bulgaria, Croatia and Romania attracted more than US$3 billion in 1999, similar to levels recorded in the previous years. The disruption to transport routes, including along the river Danube, had a detrimental impact on exporters from Bulgaria and Romania (among others) but in general, the overall effect on exports was limited.

In retrospect, the Kosovo conflict was the real turning point not just for political relations in the region but also for economic development. A new spirit of economic cooperation can be traced back to the immediate aftermath of the conflict and the promotion of regional initiatives, such as the Stability Pact for South East Europe, by the international community. As discussed in more detail below, countries in the region began to take the reform process more seriously, and, once Serbia opened up in late-2000, macroeconomic performance in the region as a whole really took off.

The new decade: sustained recovery

During the present decade, South-Eastern Europe became a region of strong economic growth. Between 2000 and 2008, no country failed to grow in any year, with the sole exception of Macedonia in 2001, when the country was paralysed for several months by a deep security crisis. Remarkably, average weighted growth in the region equalled (more or less) or exceeded that in Central-Europe and the Baltics every year between 2001 and 2008. Furthermore, this strong growth performance was combined in most cases with low inflation, as well as tangible progress in market-oriented reforms.

The region still has a lot of catching up to do, and the high growth rates of recent years should be seen in this context. This point is brought out by a comparison of the 2007 level of GDP per capita—for all its faults still probably the best indicator of economic well-being—with selected countries in Central Europe (see Table 1). Two measures of GDP are given (both in US dollars): one is a simple conversion to dollars at average market exchange rates, while the second gives an estimate in terms of purchasing power parity (PPP). That is, the latter adjusts the former figure to take account of the fact that a dollar in one country may go further in terms of what it can buy than the same dollar in another country.

Table 1: GDP per capita in 2007, nominal and PPP-adjusted, US dollars

Country	GDP per capita at average exchange rates	GDP per capita, PPP-adjusted
Albania	3354	6290
Bosnia and Herzegovina	3712	6964
Bulgaria	5186	11302
Croatia	11576	15549
Macedonia	3659	8468
Montenegro	4950	9867
Romania	7697	11387
Serbia	5596	10375

Czech Republic	17070	24236
Hungary	13762	19027
Poland	11041	16311
Slovak Republic	13857	20251
Slovenia	22933	27205

Source: IMF, World Economic Outlook, April 2008.

Whichever measure of GDP is used, the gap between South-Eastern Europe and central Europe is clear. Only Croatia comes close to reaching the standards of a country like Poland, and even Bulgaria and Romania, both now in the EU, lag well behind, as do Serbia and Montenegro. Albania remains the poorest country in South-Eastern Europe although there is little difference in GDP per capita compared to Bosnia and Herzegovina and Macedonia. It should also be noted that there is such a wide range of uncertainty around the estimates of both GDP and, in some cases (such as Bosnia and Herzegovina) population in these countries that confident statements about ranking of countries by GDP per capita are not possible.

The most encouraging feature of the region's economic performance has been the strong, sustained growth of the last 6–7 years. The average annual growth rate, weighted by the size of each economy, has never since 2001 fallen below 4.7 per cent (until 2009), and it rose as high as 7 per cent in 2004. The growth has been fairly well distributed across the region. Only Macedonia has consistently posted a GDP growth below the regional average, and even this country accelerated with an estimated 5 per cent growth in 2007. Notwithstanding this good performance, several countries still have an estimated level of GDP that is below that of 1989. On current trends, Macedonia will need a couple more years of good growth to exceed their 1989 level of economic output, and Bosnia and Herzegovina, Montenegro and Serbia will require between six and seven years. The global economic crisis has ensured that these targets will be postponed for some time (see Chapter VII for more discussion).

How can the strong growth of recent years be explained? On the demand side, consumer spending rose sharply, fuelled by an explosion of credit growth, which in turn reflected the fundamental overhaul of the region's banking systems. Credit expanded rapidly in South-Eastern Europe for a number of years, under the influence of a major improvement in the banking sector, and many individuals and households now routinely borrow from banks to fund purchases of durable goods, holidays and even house purchases. The Life in Transition Survey (on which more below) by the EBRD and World Bank, carried out in September 2006, shows that, at that time, 35 per cent of respondent households in South-Eastern Europe had at least one credit or debit card. The figure has undoubtedly risen since then. Whether this level of credit growth is sustainable in the medium- to long-term is an issue examined in detail in Chapter VI.

A second factor that drove growth was the revival of export markets. The conflicts of the 1990s had a disastrous impact on trade, both within the region and with the outside world. Within the region, there is evidence from numerous studies that cross-border trade is well below the kind of levels seen in similar size markets and regions in other parts of the world. Outside the region, the main market is the EU but although access to EU markets has been duty-free for most non-agricultural goods since 2000, in practice there are numerous obstacles to reaching these markets, such as the failure to satisfy EU quality standards. Increasingly, however, these problems are being overcome. Cross-border trade is one of the most vibrant parts of the region's economy, and the recent regional free trade agreement may help to cement the gains of recent years (we return to this issue in Chapter VI).

Turning to the supply-side, one remarkable turnaround in several countries was been the revival of certain key industries. Major investments into once moribund industries produced significant results, for example in the steel industry in Bosnia and Herzegovina, FYR Macedonia, Romania and Serbia (although this sector has been particularly hard hit by the global crisis). Arcelor-Mittal bought steel plants in Macedonia and Bosnia and Herzegovina and production in both plants for a time increased significantly, while US Steel's investment in Serbia also bore fruit until global demand collapsed. The construction industry was also booming across the region, particularly in areas where investment and new building had been lagging behind, but also in some of the capitals of the region, such as Belgrade and Bucharest.

As a result of these changes, the structure of the region's economy has shifted over the past decade away from old, dying industries and more towards services, similar to the evolution of other, more advanced emerging markets. In all countries, the share of services as a percentage of GDP is now above 50 per cent. The third main sector—agriculture—has also declined across the region as a share of GDP, although it remains a particularly important part of the economies in several countries, including Albania, Macedonia, Romania and Serbia.

Small businesses and the informal sector

A feature of most economies in the region is the prevalence of micro-, small and medium-sized enterprises (MSMEs), many of which operate informally. Life for MSMEs in South-Eastern Europe has become easier over the years, and the number of registered businesses has grown sharply in recent years. According to data from the OECD and EBRD, the number of MSMEs per 1,000 inhabitants in the early part of the decade ranged from 7.9 in Bosnia and Herzegovina to 28.7 in Bulgaria. Even the latter figure, though is well below the OECD average. The vast majority of these enterprises are micro (less than ten employees) or small (between ten and forty-nine employees), concentrated mostly in low value added sectors. All countries in the region take seriously the importance of providing the right environment for SME development. However, the quality of assistance on offer varies widely. A joint OECD-EBRD assessment in 2003 showed significant weaknesses in the institutional framework for small enterprises, especially in Bosnia and Herzegovina but also in Macedonia, Albania and Serbia.

Many SMEs carry out their business outside official channels; informal activities are also a key part of the region's economy. In this regard, South-Eastern Europe is little different from other emerging regions. Even in the most advanced countries, some individuals and enterprises operate outside the law by failing to report all of their business activities to the relevant authorities or by neglecting to obtain all the necessary licences and permits. Anecdotal evidence suggests that many businesses maintain two sets of books, one that they show to the authorities and the other which records the true state of the company's affairs. The grey economy exists in every country, but it is more likely to thrive in the kind of chaotic environment that several countries in the region experienced in the 1990s.

The informal economy can be divided into two parts: activities that are legal, or at least would be if they were fully registered and reported, and those that are illegal under any circumstances. The latter category includes organised crime, smuggling, people-trafficking, dealing in drugs and the like. This category is recognised by all governments in the region as a serious problem, and some efforts have been made to stamp it out, albeit with varying success. The problems of corruption and organised crime, and how they affect the business environment, are addressed in more detail in Chapter VI below. But there is less agreement on how to deal with the first category. Governments in the region recognise that the informal sector plays a key role in poverty alleviation, by helping those who cannot find legitimate jobs to earn some money and survive.

How big is the informal sector in South-Eastern Europe? By its very nature, it is impossible to be very precise about this. Various sophisticated ways have been used to come up with an estimate. One approach uses 'factor analysis' on a number of possible causes and indicators to estimate the size of the informal economy. Relevant indicators may include, for example, changes in cash holdings or in labour participation rates. This method leads to estimates of the informal sector that are broadly similar across South-Eastern Europe countries, at around one-third of GDP. This is somewhat higher than the typical estimate for an OECD country about 18 per cent of GDP. An alternative, and probably more reliable, method is to compare actual tax revenue can be compared with what the level of revenue should be if all enterprises paid the correct amount of tax. This method gives a much wider range of estimates.

Macroeconomic policies

In general, macroeconomic policies over the past decade in South-Eastern Europe can be characterised as prudent. Two of the main indicators of macroeconomic stability—inflation and the general government deficit—have typically been low, some at levels that would be the envy of a number of EU members. All governments and central banks in the region recognise the importance of stabilisation and low inflation for economic growth. And all know that it is not possible for these countries, which are mostly small and increasingly open economies, to try to boost economic activity over the long-term by running large fiscal deficits or by increasing inflation. But different countries have adopted different approaches to the way they run monetary and exchange rates policy, and to the size of government.

Turning first to monetary policy, one of the interesting features of the region is the wide variety of exchange rate regimes adopted by the different countries. Albania, Croatia, Romania and Serbia all float their currencies to some extent, with varying degrees of management by the central banks. All of these countries have managed to avoid sharp exchange rate fluctuations over most of the recent period, which has helped to keep inflation down and, perhaps more importantly, has reduced people's expectations of inflation. Other countries however have adopted a more self-restrained approach. Macedonia has a fixed peg policy to the euro (previously the DM) with very small room for adjustment in either direction. There have been no devaluations since July 1997, even though the central bank and the government regularly have to fight off rumours of imminent devaluation. Bosnia and Herzegovina and Bulgaria have currency boards, with the currency fixed to the euro. The authorities in Bulgaria have signalled firmly and repeatedly their intention to maintain this peg right up to the point at which the country joins the 'Eurozone'.

The most unusual case in South-Eastern Europe is that of Montenegro, which unilaterally adopted the DM in late-1999, initially as a parallel currency to the dinar and then, from late-2000, as the sole legal tender, replacing it in 2002 with the euro. This was a clever move, driven by political considerations (the desire of the regime to distance Montenegro from Serbia) but with a clear economic motivation also. However, both the European Commission and the European Central Bank have voiced their displeasure from time to time at the country's temerity in adopting the euro without even being an EU member, much less jumping through the various hurdles (the so-called 'Maastricht criteria') that new EU members have to go through before they can become part of the 'Eurozone'.

The Montenegro solution has been firmly ruled out by the European Commission for others. It remains unclear how the Commission will treat Montenegro once the time comes to negotiate membership, although it is unlikely that the country would be forced to abandon the euro and introduce its own currency. In practice, however, the whole region has become highly 'eurosised' already; large transactions tend to be priced and carried out in euros. Also, it is clear that the type of exchange rate regime chosen seems to have little effect on inflation, and it has not been possible to draw any close link with output performance. In any case, monetary policy is about more than managing the exchange rate; it also involves decisions about interest rates and reserve requirements. In most countries, both interest rates and reserve requirements have fallen over time, but they remain useful tools for central banks concerned about excessive credit growth. (We return to this issue in Chapter VI.)

The size of government varies across the region. Countries in the former Yugoslavia have a tradition of strong state revenue collection powers, leaving a legacy of large government that continues to this day. General government spending is high across all former Yugoslav countries relative to GDP compared with other countries at a comparable stage of economic development. At the other end of the scale, the collapse of communism in Albania left the country with a weak state and limited ability to collect tax revenue from firms and households. However, most countries have been largely successful in coming close to budget balance, as shown by the latest estimates for 2007, which range from a deficit of 3.2 per cent of GDP in Albania to a surplus of 3.6 per cent of GDP in Montenegro. These low fiscal deficits (or surpluses in some cases) are a sign of several things—buoyant tax collection on the back of growing economies, fiscal prudence and a lack of access to international capital markets. Most countries are now rated by some or all of the main ratings agencies but are hesitant at present to tap these markets to any great extent. The current turmoil in international capital markets (as of end-2009) suggests that this will remain the case for the time being.

External balances

While inflation and government balances are not giving much cause for concern at present, one worrying feature common to most countries is the high current account deficit. In many cases, these deficits are at double-digit levels as a percentage of GDP. For example, estimates for 2007 put the current account deficit in Serbia at 16 per cent of GDP, in Bulgaria at 21 per cent, and, highest of all, Montenegro at around 37 per cent of GDP. High current account deficits are nothing new for this region, and indeed transition economies in general have tended to have large current account deficits (with some exceptions among natural resource-rich countries). Neverthe-less, a current account deficit is an indicator of a country liv-ing beyond its means, at least temporarily, in the sense that some imports of goods and services are being paid for by some combination of sales of capital, borrowing, and running down reserves. Clearly this cannot go on for ever.

Should we be worried? Normally the answer would be yes, especially in countries that maintain fixed exchange rates. However, in the case of South-Eastern Europe, there are sev-eral mitigating factors. First, some of these estimates exagger-ate the scale of the problem, because the data fail to account properly for remittances and other transfers (see below). If these were fully incorporated, the estimate of the current account deficit in a number of countries could be reduced by several percentage points. Second, trade opportunities have greatly expanded in recent years, and most countries are showing rapidly rising exports, as lost markets are recovered. If these trends continue—and there is every reason to expect they will once the global economy improves—trade and cur-rent account deficits are likely to decline over time. And third, large current account deficits are normal in countries that are attracting major inflows of capital. The overall balance of payments in most cases looks healthy and foreign reserves across the region have been rising steadily in recent years.

One of the most encouraging signs of the region's recent progress has been the huge influx in recent years of foreign direct investment (FDI). The headline numbers are impres-sive: US$ 15 billion in 2005, US$ 28 billion in 2006 and, in 2007, a record US$ 32 billion. Estimates show that this level of investment was maintained in 2008 but fell sharply in 2009. The bulk of this is flowing to the more advanced coun-tries: Bulgaria and Romania (both now EU members) and Croatia (an EU candidate, currently in negotiations for mem-bership). Serbia has also attracted large amounts of FDI in recent years, mostly related to important privatisations and acquisitions, but inflows to other western Balkan countries have been limited. Nevertheless, the fact that such large amounts of money are flowing to the region is a welcome sign of the increasing confidence of investors. What is less encouraging, however, is the fact that FDI is increasingly going into real estate and financial services, which are less likely to generate export revenues than investments into manufacturing companies.

The role of remittances

Many citizens of South-Eastern European countries live abroad. The conflicts during the 1990s saw a large exodus of people, in particular from some of the countries of former Yugoslavia and from Albania. As a result, remittances from these migrants back to families and friends at home have soared. Most of these funds go towards the purchase of consumer goods, but increasing attention is being paid to the development role of remittances. These inflows can ease the transition to a market economy, for example, by lowering the rate of unemployment that would otherwise prevail in the country that migrant workers had left, and by allowing policy-makers to pursue a more rapid course of transition. Furthermore, remittances can help revive a spirit of entrepreneurship, which was often discouraged or even suppressed under previous governments.

South-Eastern Europe, and the western Balkans in particular, attracts large amounts of remittances each year. In 2006, data from the IMF's Balance of Payments yearbook show that Albania, Bosnia and Herzegovina, Montenegro and Serbia are all among the top twenty countries in the world in terms of remittance inflows as a percentage of GDP. The stability of these inflows suggests that remittances are likely to remain an important source of foreign currency for most countries of the region for the foreseeable future. Policy-makers across the region are examining ways in which migrant workers can be encouraged to send remittances through formal, rather than informal, channels. Not only would this more reliably reflect how much money is actually being provided, but it would help to strengthen the local banking sector and financial intermediation more generally.

A small survey in selected countries by the EBRD in 2006 highlights the importance of remittances for micro and small businesses. Among those entrepreneurs who have received remittances in the past, nearly half had used part of them to help either start up a company, or finance ongoing investment and working capital needs. Interestingly, micro enterprises appear to be less reliant on remittances for starting up businesses than small firms are, although the small sample size rules out any definitive statement on the issue. Small companies in the region tend to be older than micro enterprises, so this finding suggests that other sources of finance, such as bank lending, have become more readily available. Nevertheless, the sheer volume of remittances to the region will ensure that they continue to fill the gap for many start-ups, either in the formal or informal sector.

External debt

Most countries in South-Eastern Europe have significant amounts of external debt. Prior to the current decade, the source of credit for the region was mostly official—governments, state agencies and international financial institutions. Now the bulk of the external credit is from private sources. Mostly, the levels of external debt are relatively moderate across the region, but looking simply at the aggregate data can be misleading. Private debt is often fuelled by lending from western parent banks to their subsidiaries in the region. There is increasing concern about how these banks might react if conditions deteriorated in the destination country. Related to this vulnerability is the fact that a significant majority of credit to the non-government sector is either directly in foreign currency or is indexed to foreign currency (in both cases, usually the euro). The liabilities side of banks' balance sheets, however, are dominated by local currency. This mismatch means that banks could face a large number of defaults if the local currency were to depreciate sharply (in the case of floating currencies) or be devalued (in the fixed case).

Awareness of these risks has been heightened during 2008 and the first half of 2009 as banks around the world faced severe difficulties associated with tighter liquidity, deteriorating loan portfolios and a need to attract fresh capital. In general the risks appear to be manageable, not least because parent banks have committed publicly in a number of countries to maintaining support for their subsidiaries (see chapters VI and VII for more discussion).

Structural reforms

One lesson that has emerged after nearly twenty years of transition is that long-term economic success requires a fundamental turnaround in the whole structure of the economy. There is still a debate about the best approach to creating a well-functioning market economy. What works and what does not in transition? How should the state best perform its role in a private sector-driven economy? These are questions that continue to attract debate and controversy. But few would argue now that the old system of state control can deliver growth and prosperity. In South-Eastern Europe, all countries have accepted the need to move the transition forward to a market-oriented economy.

The pace of reform in the region has been mixed; the variation within this region is greater than in other transition regions. In thinking about this region, it is sometimes useful to divide it into two groups: an advanced group of reformers—Bulgaria, Romania and Croatia—and a group of less advanced countries—Albania, Bosnia and Herzegovina, Macedonia, Montenegro and Serbia—where much more needs to be done. The members of the former group are either in the EU (Bulgaria and Romania) or currently in negotiations (Croatia). The lure of the EU has been perhaps the strongest driver of reforms across transition countries. Bulgaria and Romania had been lagging behind in the late-1990s, partly influenced by the macroeconomic crises both countries suffered at the time (see above), but once there was a clear prospect of membership, the reforms accelerated. Croatia has made steady progress in reforms over the years and has long been considered an advanced transition country, with a level of transition and economic development similar to countries in central Europe. In some ways, all three countries are more market-oriented than Slovenia, an EU member since May 2004 but one where the state has retained a controlling stake and role in a number of key enterprises and banks.

Any evaluation of how far countries have gone in transition requires a methodological framework. The one adopted here is one of the most commonly used measures of transition—the EBRD transition scores. Every year the EBRD tracks reform developments across all countries in which it invests through a set of nine transition indicators covering three stages of reform: market-enabling, market-deepening and market-sustaining. *Market-enabling* reforms are those that countries usually do first, since they are the easiest and quickest to implement. They include price liberalisation, trade and foreign exchange liberalisation, and privatisation of small enterprises. *Market-deepening* reforms typically come later and refer to the privatisation of large companies and assets, and the strengthening of financial institutions both in the banking sector and in other, non-banking institutions such as leasing, pensions and equity funds. *Market-sustaining* reforms are the most difficult to carry out. On the EBRD classification, these are governance and enterprises reform, competition policy and infrastructure reform in five sectors—electricity, railways, roads, telecommunications, and water and waste water—covering such issues as commercialisation, tariff reform, quality of the regulatory framework and involvement of the private sector.

Each EBRD indicator is measured on a scale of 1 to 4+, where 1 represents little or no change from a rigid centrally planned economy and 4+ represents the standards of an industrialised market economy. The score assigned is based as far as possible on an objective judgement of reforms achieved and implemented and overall progress made in moving towards a market-driven economy. Nevertheless, some element of sub-jectivity is inevitable, and the scores often provoke heated debate in the countries themselves. No country likes to be seen as doing 'worse' than its neighbours. It is often forgotten in this debate that the scores represent just rough indicators of where a country stands in the transition path, and that many of the nuances of transition are lost in the process. These points should be borne in mind in the following discussion.

Chart 1 below shows the average transition score for each country in transition, enabling a comparison of South-Eastern Europe with other transition regions (central eastern Europe and the Baltic states, and the Commonwealth of Independent States plus Mongolia). Several interesting points emerge from this comparison. According to these criteria, Bulgaria, Croatia and Romania have all reached a level of transition close to the Central European and Baltic average. In contrast, the rest of the region lags behind, and these countries show much more variation among themselves. Leading this group is Mac-edonia, an EU candidate, followed by Albania, and then the laggards in transition—Montenegro, Bosnia and Herzegovina and Serbia. Perhaps surprisingly, the latter three countries score worse than a number of CIS countries in terms of progress in transition. When one recalls the late start to tran-sition of these three, the surprise is diminished, but perhaps not completely eliminated.

Chart 1 suggests that there is a close link between overall progress in transition and integration with the EU. Looking at the speed of reform in the 1990s and the first half of the present decade, it is clear that countries have a strong incen-tive to reform once they see a clear benefit in doing so. The EU 'anchor' is perhaps the best incentive that could have been offered to the region, and its value is obvious in the case of Bulgaria and Romania. Reforms in both countries took off in the period 2001–2004, when it became clear that each country had a clear perspective of membership within the next few years. Today, in both Bulgaria and Romania, privatisation is close to completion, financial sector reform is well advanced and standards of competition and governance have been transformed. There was a slowdown in 2004–2005 after both countries had completed negotiations on all chapters of the EU's *acquis communautaire*. However, strong pressure from the European Commission to adhere to the original target date of January 1, 2007 pushed both countries to redouble their efforts during 2005 and 2006. Meanwhile, Croatia has long been regarded as an 'advanced' transition country and, in many ways, belongs with the Central European group in terms of its transition achievements. The period in the run-up to, and following, the attainment of formal candidate status with the

Chart 1: Average EBRD Transition Score, 2007

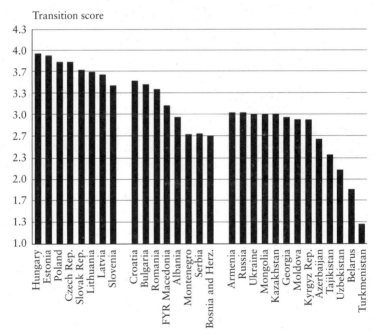

Note: The transition indicators range from 1 to 4+ (shown in the chart as 4.3), with 1 representing little or no change from a rigid centrally planned economy and 4+ (4.3) representing the standards of an industrialised market economy.

Source: EBRD.

EU was a particularly fruitful one for reforms, especially in banking, large-scale privatisation and infrastructure.

In the rest of the region, transition has been harder to push forward. The leaders in this group are Macedonia and Albania, both of which started their transition around 1991. In many ways, both countries have done their best in difficult circumstances but have been held back (especially Albania) by weak institutions and a lack of implementation capacity. Nevertheless, the first-phase, market-enabling reforms are more or less complete. For example, both countries are members of the World Trade Organisation (not yet true for the other three countries in the region). Encouragingly, the serious security crises that erupted in both countries—in 1997 in Albania and in 2001 in Macedonia—(not to mention the spillover effects of Kosovo in 1999) did not derail the reform efforts. More recently, both countries are pushing ahead, sometimes slowly, with deeper reforms to governance, competition policy and infrastructure. These reforms are likely to take much longer than they did in countries like Bulgaria and Romania, but the experience of small countries such as those in the Baltic region shows that they can be done.

In Bosnia and Herzegovina, Montenegro and Serbia, the whole transition has been overshadowed by the legacy of the violent break-up of Yugoslavia. Transition began in Bosnia and Herzegovina in 1996, but it was some years before any kind of genuine 'local ownership' of reforms took root. The whole process has been a frustrating one in Bosnia and Herzegovina. The main success story is probably the banking sector, which is well capitalised and highly competitive, with strong foreign banks competing aggressively for market share. But there is still a significant privatisation agenda ahead, and while the Republika Srpska has made much progress recently, attracting large sums of money for flagship sales in the telecoms and oil sectors, the process in the Federation is mostly stuck. There is a growing conviction in Bosnia and Herzegovina that constitutional reform is vital not just for political reasons but also for putting the reform process back on track. How this can be achieved in the present climate, however, is unclear.

ECONOMIC RECOVERY AND REFORMS

Transition in Montenegro and Serbia has followed different paths since the late-1990s, when the Đukanovic regime in Montenegro began to distance itself from Belgrade. In many ways, Montenegro has made impressive progress in transition given the limitations (in terms of administrative capacity) of the state. The country entered independence with an economy that is liberal in some areas such as trade policy and small-scale privatisation (which was effectively completed several years ago), but at an early stage of reform regarding institutions and infrastructure. Banking sector reform has progressed significantly and the sector is now in private hands. The high growth that the country is now enjoying and the recent boost from the EU (notably the signing of the Stabilisation and Association Agreement in October 2007 and the country's subsequent application for membership in April 2009) give encouragement that reforms can be pushed ahead in future years, with support from the EU and other international organisations.

Meanwhile, in Serbia, the transition has been somewhat 'stop-go'. Serbia is a country with great potential and, when transition finally got underway in late-2000, the conditions looked right for the country to make up quickly for lost time. During the first couple of years, the progress in reform was indeed rapid. Serbia was singled out by the EBRD and other IFIs for special praise in terms of *progress* in reform. In the initial euphoria, the fact that it was starting from such a low base was sometimes forgotten. The energy and charisma of Prime Minister Zoran Đinđić and his team of dynamic young reformers captured the imagination, if not of the Serbian people (who largely distrusted Đinđić while he was alive), at least of the international community. The country quickly implemented comprehensive liberalisation of many prices and trade barriers, it initiated a privatisation programme with an emphasis on attracting outside investment, and it began a fundamental overhaul of the banking system.

The assassination of Đinđić in March 2003 was a huge blow to the reform process. The rest of that year and much of the following year was a lost period of pre-election bickering and post-election manoeuvring, until a new coalition government was formed, led by Vojislav Koštunica. Few people had high expectations of this government, and many expected it to fall quickly, but in fact it managed to achieve quite a lot on the reform front. During 2005 and 2006 Serbia was once again among the leaders of reform throughout the whole transition region. However, politics since then have slowed down the process once more. In 2007 and early 2008, the political agenda has been overshadowed by the lengthy negotiations to form a government, a process that lasted nearly four months, and by the Kosovo status issue, which for a time dominated the government's policy agenda. Transition is still advancing in Serbia but the country's ambition to lead the region in reform currently depends on whether the multi–party coalition government, formed after parliamentary elections on May 11, 2008, manages to function effectively and cohesively. The evidence so far is rather mixed.

Reform resistance and attitudes to transition

The reforms implemented in South-Eastern Europe have brought considerable benefits to people living in the region. Without these reforms, the high growth rates of recent years would not have been possible. This point is brought out by recent research that shows a strong and robust positive link between reforms, as measured by the EBRD indicators described above, and growth. According to this research, an upgrade in three 'transition indicators' in a given year can increase a country's growth rate by about one percentage point, and provided there is no backtracking in the future, this rate of growth can be maintained over a longer period.

It seems safe to assert that there is no great appetite within any part of the region for a return to the former economic system. In most countries, political debate is dominated by non-economic issues. Governments and central banks in the region generally accept the need for macroeconomic stabilisation and market-oriented reforms. Very few people would argue that pro-market reforms are not good for growth, or that there is a serious alternative to the present policies. However, the approach to reform has been hesitant at times. In the case of Bulgaria and Romania, there has been a noticeable slowdown in reform since accession to the EU was confirmed in 2006. Both countries have a significant agenda of third-phase reforms ahead but show little appetite at present for such a course. The EU Council reports, adopted in June 2007, were quite critical of both countries for insufficient progress in areas such as tackling corruption and (in the case of Bulgaria) organised crime. As noted earlier, the July 2008 reports essentially reiterated the same messages. Elsewhere, the reform agenda is often neglected when more pressing issues (from the point of view of politicians) come into play.

Why have the reforms not gone faster in the region? One explanation might be that people are fed up with reforms and the effects the transition has had on their lives. It has been recognised for some time that transition has been a difficult experience for many people, but until recently there was no comprehensive survey of individuals' attitudes and experiences across the whole transition region. This is no longer the case; in 2006, the EBRD and the World Bank jointly carried out a 'Life in Transition survey' (LiTS) of 29,000 individuals in twenty-eight transition countries plus Turkey (1,000 people per country). People were asked a range of questions about, *inter alia*, their experience of transition over the previous fifteen years or so, their attitudes to markets and democracy, their overall life satisfaction today and their view on public services and institutions, corruption and trust. The results provide a fascinating insight into how people view the transition process and the way it has shaped their lives.

The most striking thing about the results in South-Eastern Europe is how unhappy people are in this region relative to the other two regions, and how few people think that things are better today than they were in 1989. Chart 2 illustrates the latter point. Across the region, there is a widespread view that things were better back in 1989. An examination of the country-level data shows that this effect is strongest in most former Yugoslav republics (Bosnia and Herzegovina, Macedonia, Montenegro and Serbia), where people overwhelmingly believe that the economic and political situations were better under the old regime (people in Croatia and Slovenia have a more favourable view). Such results are not surprising, given the relative prosperity that people in the former Yugoslavia enjoyed before the country's break-up. More puzzling, perhaps, is the fact that a majority of people in Bulgaria and Romania also hold the same view. In contrast, Albanians tend to regard transition in a much more positive light, no doubt remembering the bleak economic conditions and oppressive political regime that prevailed up to the end of the 1980s.

Chart 3 highlights the high degree of dissatisfaction in South-Eastern Europe. Objectively, people in the region have much to be unhappy about. As noted earlier, in four countries

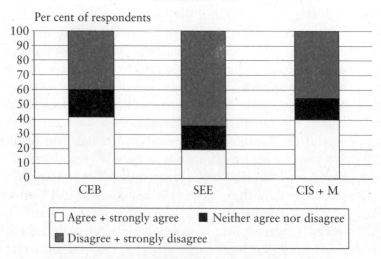

Chart 2: Views on the Economic Situation

The econonic situation in this country is better today
than around 1989

Per cent of respondents

Source: EBRD/World Bank Life in Transition Survey.

of the region (Bosnia and Herzegovina, Macedonia, Montenegro, and Serbia), real GDP is still below 1989 levels. And GDP is by no means a sure guide to individual well-being and happiness. For many people, transition has been associated with uncertainty and worry, about issues ranging from fear of losing one's job to being unable to pay higher electricity bills, or falling ill and being subjected to the vagaries and petty corruption of the state-run health system. As a result, self-reported life satisfaction is significantly lower in South-Eastern Europe than in Central Europe and Baltic states or the Commonwealth of Independent States. These facts have to be borne in mind by policy-makers, who know that reforms are often painful initially, with the benefits coming only later. When people are already miserable it can become impossible for policy makers to push through further reforms, whatever the applause and encouragement from foreign institutions and investors on the sidelines. One encouraging result from the LiTS, however, is the confirmation of the lack of enthusi-

Chart 3: Life Satisfaction, by Region

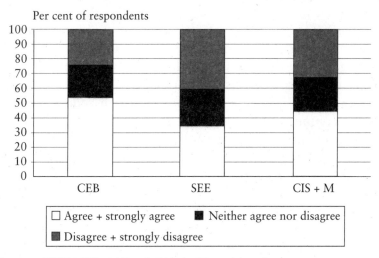

Source: EBRD/World Bank Life in Transition Survey.

asm for any return to a planned economy or an authoritarian political regime.

Concluding remarks

South-Eastern Europe has come a long way since 1990. The transition path has been anything but smooth—the 1990s is a decade that is probably best forgotten as far as most people living in the region are concerned. But important lessons were learned in this decade, especially the need for a sustained commitment to reforms rather than searching for a quick fix. This chapter has summarised the main economic developments over the past two decades. It is a complicated story, full of ups and downs and wide differences across countries. But a number of common themes have emerged, and three are worth emphasising here.

The first lesson is that macroeconomic stabilisation is crucial for economic growth. Some countries had to learn this the hard way, since an initial period of economic growth was not backed up by sound macroeconomic policies. Now, low inflation and low fiscal deficits are pretty firmly entrenched in the region, and very people would try to argue that countries like these can spend their way to higher growth and prosperity. The main concern as of end-2009 is how to mitigate the effects of the global economic crisis, and several countries in the region have already sought the help of the IMF and other international institutions in this regard.

The second lesson is that strong growth requires a sustained commitment to reforms. There is a clear correlation between countries that have advanced furthest in reforms and those that have grown fastest in recent years. Increasingly, reforms are focusing on building institutions that can sustain market interactions. The EU perspective for the region is crucial in keeping those countries that are not yet members, or even candidates, focused on reforms.

The final lesson is that people are highly impatient for better times. Those who grew up in the former Yugoslavia remember a time when they lived well and could travel freely abroad. Bulgarians and Romanians recognise that their living standards lag behind the rest of the EU and they would like to close the gap as much as possible. Only in Albania, it seems (according to survey evidence), do people perceive their situation to be significantly better than before transition, and the degree of impatience there may not be as high here as elsewhere. This impatience is an opportunity and a threat to policymakers in the region—an opportunity because it creates a sense of urgency in trying to improve people's lot, but also a threat because there may be a reluctance to push ahead with potentially painful reforms. The next chapter evaluates how the region's strong entrepreneurial spirit and reform momentum can be harnessed to ensure long-term prosperity.

6

FROM AID TO TRADE AND INVESTMENT

Recapturing the momentum

South-Eastern Europe became a region of strong growth during the first decade of the new millennium, but the decade is ending with a return to recession as the region faces the full effects of the global economic crisis. Notwithstanding these short-term problems (which are discussed in more detail in the final chapter) the region has potential to resume rapid growth over the medium-term. But how likely is it that the growth momentum can be recaptured, and what are the main risks? These questions are analysed in this chapter, which comes up with an assessment of future prospects that is both optimistic and realistic. The answers to these questions cannot be definitive. Consistent growth over the long-term depends on a variety of factors: sound macroeconomic management, a sustained commitment to structural reforms, openness to trade and investment, and finally luck. There is little that countries in the region can do to affect the last requirement, but much that can be, and still needs to be, done about the others. What makes predictions difficult is that one cannot be sure that each country will keep on track with reforms, but one can at least be confident that there will be no serious back-tracking. Among the many reasons why we believe that economies in South-Eastern Europe can continue to grow, two are worth mentioning up front.

The first is the fact that the region still has a long way to go to catch up on central European and Baltic states. Not only is average GDP per capita well below that of the typical country in central Europe and the Baltic states, as noted in the previous chapter, but in four of the eight countries, GDP is still below estimated 1989 levels, measured in constant currency. Even the two EU members of the region—Bulgaria and Romania—have a GDP per capita well below half (in purchasing power parity terms) the EU average. The second reason is that all countries will, we believe, eventually be part of the European Union. Whatever its weaknesses, the EU has an unparalleled success rate in promoting prosperity among its members, not just after membership is secured but even beforehand, because the prize of membership, once it is clear that it will be attained, is a powerful draw for investors.

The private sector already dominates economic activity in the region and will continue to do so. Consider a potential business person or investor (either domestic or foreign) in the region; what are the kinds of things that will give him/her confidence to set up or expand a business? One key factor is political stability. Previous chapters have shown how this has developed and matured over time and have argued that, despite remaining problems besetting parts of the region, there will be no return to the dark days of the 1990s. But the hypothetical business person, even if reassured about the region's political prospects, will want the answers to some other fundamental questions. Will macroeconomic policies be appropriate for promoting growth? Will the authorities take firm action to improve the business environment? Will finance be readily available for new business opportunities and will banks and other financial institutions work properly? Will there be easy access to international markets? And will there be real investment opportunities, with the appropriate incentives and human capital available to make a profit? These are the questions that we try to answer below.

FROM AID TO TRADE AND INVESTMENT

Macroeconomic management

One of the most remarkable achievements of the region over the present decade has been the combination of strong growth (until 2009), low inflation and fiscal prudence. Once global conditions improve, it would be tempting to assume that these three characteristics will resume, at least up to the point when all countries are members of the European Union. This is certainly a possibility. But the challenges of macroeconomic policy are different today from those addressed successfully in the past. The question is whether governments and the central banks have the capacity to design and implement appropriate fiscal and monetary policies in the new circumstances.

Policy-making is more challenging for governments in the region than it used to be. One reason is that the region is increasingly open to negative spillovers, as shown by the fact that the general global downturn that began in the second half of 2007 and intensified in 2008 hit South-Eastern Europe with full force in the first half of 2009 (see Chapter VII below). Another reason is that the importance of the IMF has evolved over time. For several years, the IMF had been withdrawing gradually from the region, before reversing dramatically in 2009 to play a key role in several countries' crisis-response programmes. It remains unclear, however, whether there will be a role for the IMF once the region starts to recover from the crisis. The EU anchor is important for structural reforms but does not provide the same kind of IMF-driven straitjacket when it comes to macroeconomic policy. In other words, over the medium term when growth returns, the opportunities for more spending will be greater than before, but the capacity to exercise these opportunities may not be in place.

Fiscal policy

For most people, a 'good' fiscal policy is usually equated with a balanced budget. This is implicit in one of the so-called Maastricht criteria for membership of the 'Eurozone', which states that the general government balance should be zero over the long-term, and no more than 3 per cent in deficit (relative to GDP) in any one year. Most countries in the region have shown that they can stay within this limit, but this has been under relatively benign macroeconomic circumstances. In the more difficult environment of 2008/09, things are not so easy, regardless of when each country is likely to enter the 'Eurozone'. There are constant pressures on governments to spend more. We know from the Life in Transition Survey (LiTS), discussed in the previous chapter, that many people in South-Eastern Europe are highly dissatisfied with life and impatient for improvements, especially in public services and infrastructure. Over the medium and long term, all of these countries will face the familiar problem of aging populations, possibly made worse by emigration of mostly younger people, thus increasing the dependency ratio.

Bulgaria and Romania, as members of the EU, are committed to adhering to the principles of the 1992 Maastricht Treaty, even though membership of the second phase of the Exchange Rate Mechanism (ERM-II) is probably some years away. Both countries have strong investment needs to upgrade infrastructure to the standards of other EU countries, and this will force major spending on the governments for some years to come. The availability of EU structural funds will alleviate, but not completely eliminate, this pressure. However, the two countries face quite distinct fiscal challenges.

On the surface, Bulgaria appears to be performing better than Romania from a fiscal standpoint. The general government budget in Bulgaria was a 3.5 per cent surplus in 2007, whereas Romania was in deficit by 2.5 per cent. In early 2008, the European Commission explicitly warned Romania that it might face the European Commission's 'excessive deficit procedure'; the government responded by announcing a set of spending freezes and cutbacks, as well as a cap on public sector wage increases, to try to reduce the planned deficit for 2008 from 2.9 per cent of GDP, which was far too close to the edge for the Commission's liking, to 2.5 per cent of GDP. But the apparent divergence between the two countries must be put in context of two factors—the exchange rate regime and the current account deficit. Bulgaria continues to run a currency board and intends to do so up to the point when the country can enter the 'Eurozone', while Romania has a floating exchange rate, although subject to some management by the central bank.

The comparison of fiscal policy in Bulgaria and Romania highlights an important macroeconomic principle: a country that eliminates one important lever of macroeconomic policy by adopting a rigid currency peg (as exemplified by the currency board) must be extra careful of its fiscal position. Any weakness on the fiscal side may persuade markets that the currency board is vulnerable, and the experience of currency board collapses in other countries shows that the results can be swift and brutal. Related to this is the fact that Bulgaria was running an even higher current account deficit than Romania—21 per cent versus 14 per cent of GDP in 2007. Again, markets are looking to see that this enormous deficit of private saving is compensated to some extent by a surplus of public saving. Finally, Bulgaria's public debt is higher than Romania's (20.8 versus 13 per cent of GDP in 2007), which acts as a further constraint on building up new public debt through fiscal deficits.

Elsewhere in the region, the Maastricht requirements are more a theoretical than practical consideration at this point, but many of the fiscal challenges are similar. As noted, most countries have managed to keep a lid on public spending, although it remains high in most countries of the western Balkans (with the exception of Albania) compared to other countries of similar economic development. The revenue-gathering capabilities have been improved by reforms such as the introduction of VAT and the gradual formalisation of economic activities.

Can this fiscal discipline be maintained? It is difficult to be sure, especially as the temptations are likely to grow over time. Some countries in this part of the region have had little choice but to maintain a balanced, or close to balanced, budget. One reason is that many of them had IMF programmes where they committed to a strong degree of fiscal discipline. Another is that alternative sources of funding were simply not available, but this situation is changing gradually, bringing both new opportunities and associated risks. Take the case of Bosnia and Herzegovina, for example. Until recently the country had no international rating, so access to foreign borrowing, other than official loans (often for post-war reconstruction efforts) was limited or non-existent. Meanwhile, on the domestic front, there was no market for government debt. Hence, the only way governments (at entity or state level) could run deficits was through arrears on public obligations such as wages and pensions. Now the situation has changed—governments at all levels in BH have a greater capacity to borrow, and tapping international capital markets is now on the cards since the government has achieved a rating from Moody's credit rating agency. It remains to be seen whether the temptation to tap these new sources of credit, in a country where the fiscal architecture is still complicated and coordination of fiscal policy is weak, will be resisted. In this regard, the introduction of a National Fiscal Council, which started functioning in the second half of 2008, is a welcome step as it enables a better coordination of spending decisions among the state, entities and cantons.

Monetary policy

Monetary policy in South-Eastern Europe involves a number of complex, inter-related decisions. Perhaps the first point to make is one of encouragement; throughout the region, decisions about monetary policy are clearly in the hands of the respective central banks. Politicians have generally interfered less in this area than might have been feared. The good news is that, without exception, central banks in the region have established a strong reputation for professionalism and competence. Salaries for those working at the central bank are generally well above those for other public sector jobs, and this has helped to recruit and retain qualified and dedicated staff. These people have their work cut out for them; just as with fiscal policy, there are new challenges ahead that central banks in the region have not faced before, and little consensus at present about how best to address them.

For the first time in years, the whole region experienced strong inflationary pressures in the first half of 2008. In response to this, some central banks broadly maintained their stance on foreign exchange rate mechanisms and have fought inflation through a combination of interest-rate increases and often stringent reserve requirements. Interest rates were raised aggressively in several countries in late-2007 and early-2008, notably in Romania and Serbia, in an effort to contain credit growth. Theses trends were reversed in 2009 when inflation receded as a threat but recession became the main headache (see Chapter VII below). Regarding reserve requirements, there was no consensus of approach, with a range in early-2008 of requirements on foreign reserves range from 10 per cent in Albania and FYR Macedonia to 45 per cent in Serbia. Interestingly, reserve requirements tend to be higher in countries with a floating exchange rate regime. It is not clear why this should be the case. One possibility is that these countries have been less successful in fighting inflation, and therefore central banks are more reluctant to be seen to show any weakness on one key plank of monetary policy.

Different central banks have adopted very different approaches to issues such as inflation targeting, exchange rate policy and reserve requirements. In itself, this is not a problem, since there are different ways of getting to the same objectives of price stability and sustainable credit growth. The previous chapter showed that exchange rate policies in the region range from unilateral euro adoption in Montenegro to the managed float regime in several other countries, such as Albania, Croatia and Serbia. It is not possible to attribute economic success or failure to the choice of exchange rate regime; other factors are far more important as long-run determinants. But this does not mean that the choice of regime is irrelevant. The wrong exchange rate policy, combined with other inappropriate policies and/or bad luck, can have serious negative consequences in the short-run. The important point for central bankers in the region is that the right policy mix for stabilising the economy in the past may no longer be appropriate in the future.

Given the high degree of European influence that already exists throughout the region, one might ask why more countries do not contemplate a unilateral adoption of the euro, as Montenegro has done. From a purely theoretical perspective, there are many attractions to such a policy. It certainly seems to suit Montenegro, in terms of delivering stability and low inflation (although rising in 2008), as well as taking the inconvenience out of exchange rate conversion for tourists from the 'Eurozone'. The problem for any other country taking such a step is that both the European Commission and the European Central Bank have firmly closed this particular door. Both institutions are unhappy that Montenegro has simply bypassed the elaborate steps and hurdles that new EU members must pass through before being deemed fit to join the euro club. However, there is little they can do about it at this stage; it does not seem realistic to force Montenegro, as a condition of EU membership, to introduce a domestic currency. Montenegro's small size is an advantage in this respect; a bigger country would probably not be treated so leniently. The euro is also *de facto* the only currency in use throughout most of Kosovo.

For those other countries that have chosen hard pegs—Bosnia and Herzegovina and Bulgaria with their currency boards, and Macedonia with a fixed peg—there are risks to continuation of this policy. One risk—more theoretical than real as of mid-2009—is that high growth in these countries will be accompanied by high inflation well beyond 'Eurozone' levels. According to the 'Balassa-Samuelson' effect, countries with fast-growing productivity in the traded sector will tend to see its real exchange rate appreciating, and if the currency is fixed, this appreciation must come through prices. This effect was already noticeable (before the crisis took hold) in several EU members with currency boards, such as Estonia and Lithuania. Provided strong growth returns to the region, this will complicate the objective of bringing inflation down to the limit specified under the Maastricht criteria.

Another risk to a hard peg policy is more immediate in the current global financial crisis. Some banks may run into short-term liquidity difficulties, particularly subsidiaries of western banks that may themselves be in financial trouble in their home countries. The hard peg policy rules out any direct relief from the central bank. In such circumstances, the risk of a general banking sector crisis is exacerbated. It would be wrong to exaggerate these risks. As discussed below, the banking sector in the region is largely well capitalised and increasingly well regulated. However, there remains the possibility that central bankers in hard peg countries of the region will have cause to regret the monetary strait-jacket they find themselves in.

Finally, there are key risks on the external side that may call for more exchange rate flexibility. High current account deficits are pervasive in the region, and at double-digit levels (as a percentage of GDP) in many cases. Historically, deficits of this magnitude have often been a cause of alarm, because they can be a leading indicator of a balance of payments crisis. However, many transition countries, in central Europe and the Baltic states as well as in South-Eastern Europe, have run large current account deficits for many years. One should not be surprised to see double-digit current account deficits in fast-growing, recovering economies with major investment needs. But this point is often not well understood by markets, which become nervous about persistently large deficits. A belief that a balance of payments crisis is on the way can be self-fulfilling. The problem for hard peg countries is that substantial reserves can be lost in trying to defend the currency, and if this defence fails, the subsequent devaluation and associated real costs can be devastating.

All of these considerations imply that countries with a hard peg must consider carefully whether or not to introduce some flexibility before the ultimate step of 'Eurozone' membership. This is a very difficult choice. Historically, there are many cases of currency boards failing, and few examples of a successful conversion of a currency board into a broader currency club. On the other side of the argument, it is hard to see how a shift towards more flexibility can be explained to the public without it seeming like an admission of weakness, and hence an excuse to abandon the domestic currency, thereby contributing to a rapid devaluation. Whatever the choice, it is essential that fiscal and monetary policy makers are working, and seen to be working, towards the same ultimate goals of macroeconomic stability and growth. The hope, and indeed the expectation, is that this lesson will be appreciated before it is too late.

Business environment

Much attention has been given in recent years to the quality of the business environment and how it affects economic growth. The private sector now dominates economic activity in the region and private firms enter and exit the market in a similar way to advanced market economies. However, businesses face a number of obstacles, such as inefficient and corrupt bureaucrats, limited access to finance, and the poor quality of public infrastructure and services. In this respect, there is nothing unique about South-Eastern Europe; all over the world, it is not hard to find business people who complain about the external problems they face in running their operations. The question is whether the situation is any worse in South-Eastern Europe than in other regions, and if so, what are governments doing about it. To answer this, we draw on various surveys both of individuals' perceptions of the business environment and of objective measures, such as the time needed to open a business, the number of licences required, the quality of investor protection, and related matters.

Subjective measures—the BEEPS

One way of finding out about the business environment is to ask the opinion of those who know most about it—business people themselves. This is the approach the EBRD and World Bank have adopted jointly over a number of years through the Business Environment and Enterprise Performance Survey (BEEPS). The BEEPS is a multi–country survey which has been carried out four times—1999, 2002, 2005, and 2008/09. It is carried out across virtually all of the transition region, and has been extended to selected non-transition countries. In 2008/09, the survey covered nearly 12,000 firms across the transition region, including 2664 firms in South-Eastern Europe. The survey contains objective information about the firm's size and turnover, but both measured as ranges to help preserve anonymity.

The main focus of attention has been on the subjective estimates by survey respondents of the severity of obstacles to doing business. Specifically, those interviewed were asked to rate a number of potential obstacles, such as macroeconomic instability, poor infrastructure quality, lack of access to finance, crime and corruption, on a scale of 0 to 4, where 0 would indicate no problem, and 4 represents a very severe problem. The same questions have been asked (sometimes with minor modifications—for example, previous rounds had a four-point rather than five-point response scale) each time, allowing both a comparison across countries and regions within the same year as well as an evaluation of progress over time.

Overall, the quality of the business environment in South-Eastern Europe appears to lag behind countries in Central Europe and the Baltic states. It is important to qualify this statement immediately by noting, first, the wide variation within the region, and second, the fact that any aggregation of the BEEPS results to come up with some kind of summary business environment measure is bound to be arbitrary. In any case, it would be wrong to take too gloomy a picture from the BEEPS about the business climate in South-Eastern Europe. For a start, most countries have progressed in the

169

more recent rounds relative to 1999 and 2002. Nevertheless, the BEEPS does highlight the extent to which more progress is needed, as well as the urgency of implementing, rather than simply passing, business-friendly reforms.

One area where parts of the region score particularly badly is in the area of corruption. The Life in Transition Survey brought out issues of petty corruption in areas such as health services and road police. Transparency International's Corruption Perceptions Index, updated annually, also paints many of these countries in an unflattering light. The BEEPS highlights the 'grasping hand' of bureaucrats in terms of excessive and intrusive inspections and demands for bribes. In 2005, several countries in the western Balkans, notably Albania, Macedonia, and Serbia and Montenegro (still one country at the time of the last survey) stand out as having severe problems of corruption. Two measures highlight this point: the 'bribe tax' and the 'time tax'. The former measures the percentage of turnover that firms have to pay each year in bribes to public officials, while the latter captures the amount of time that senior managers spend in dealing with inspections, licences, official enquiries and related matters. In the first category, the worst countries across the whole transition region were Albania, Bosnia and Herzegovina and Serbia/Montenegro, while the same countries also score quite badly in the second category. Taken together, these impediments are a major drain on the resources of companies, especially small and medium enterprises, and a big disincentive to new firms to enter the market.

Objective measures

An alternative approach to measuring and comparing the quality of the business environment is to gather hard data on concrete measures of practical matters such as the number of days needed to set up a business, the number of licences needed, the degree of contract enforcement and such like. In recent years, the World Bank has set up a comprehensive annual database, now covering 181 countries worldwide, known as the 'Doing Business' indicators. This is a valuable and increasingly used resource that complements the subjective measures gathered by the BEEPS by giving a different perspective on the problems the region faces. Since it is updated annually, it enables us to see which countries are making progress on a year-by-year basis.

Recent results ('Doing Business 2010') published in September 2009, show that, in terms of overall ease of doing business, the two EU countries, Bulgaria and Romania, stand out as strong performers in South-Eastern Europe at 44th and 55th place respectively. Interestingly, Macedonia scores best in the region at 32nd place. These three countries are followed by Montenegro, Albania and Serbia (71st, 82nd and 88th places respectively) and then, surprisingly lowly ranked, Croatia at 103rd. Bosnia and Herzegovina brings up the rear at 116th place. An examination of selected sub-components of the overall index enables one to single out particular areas of weakness. Problems of contract enforcement and dealing with licences are pervasive across the region. In contrast, there is wide variation in the level of investor protection, with Montenegro coming out particularly well, followed by Bulgaria and Romania.

What can we interpret from these results and what are governments doing to improve the situation? The picture that emerges from both studies (BEEPS and Doing Business) is broadly consistent, although there are important differences. For example, there is something of a disconnect between the apparent progress on concrete issues such as number of days and associated costs to register a business and subjective perceptions of petty corruption. However, governments increasingly take these surveys seriously. The publication of major surveys by institutions such as the World Bank and the EBRD are given widespread publicity, and any perceived progress is trumpeted loudly by the relevant authorities (low scores and criticisms are, not surprisingly, given less prominence). Also, business and foreign investor associations have generally become more vocal in their demands and criticisms, and it has become harder for governments to ignore them.

One interesting development of recent years has been the growing peer pressure among countries in the region to be seen to do something about their business climate. This process is most visible within the OCED-led Investment Compact (IC) for South-Eastern Europe. The IC is an initiative initially under the general umbrella of the Stability Pact and provides a forum within which countries from the region can work together, with the support of the OECD and other international institutions and bilateral donors, on common areas of interest for investment policy. A new IC initiative began a couple of years ago to analyse more explicitly a number of reforms, and to construct an 'investment reform index', on a scale of 1 to 5, for seven different aspects of the reform agenda. The most recent results show Bulgaria and Romania above the average for the region in all aspects, whereas Albania, Bosnia and Herzegovina and Macedonia lag behind.

The Investment Compact has played an important role in promoting dialogue among the countries of the region about investment climate issues and in encouraging the introduction of best practice on issues such as taxation of VAT, access to finance for SMEs and competition policy. It has also drawn on the lessons of business environment surveys such as those discussed above. The investment reform index is a logical extension of this process; the widespread consultation process gives countries a sense of involvement and ownership, rather than the feeling of being lectured to by international organisations. This is contributing to the growing sense that South-Eastern Europe is increasingly open for business and that the situation is much better across the board than it was a decade ago. However, the need to attract consensus can lead to a watering-down of some of the stronger conclusions.

Access to finance

One of the biggest constraints on economic development in the region has been the lack of access to finance for starting and building up a business. However, the situation in the region has changed dramatically in this respect during the present decade. Businesses routinely apply for and receive loans from banks, and non-bank institutions such as leasing institutions, pension funds and equity funds have also grown rapidly. This section considers the current state of financial intermediation and assesses how it is likely to develop in the coming years.

The banking sector

The banking sector in South-Eastern Europe has been transformed over the past ten years. The legacy of the past for financial intermediation was described briefly in the last chapter; suffice to say here that the opening circumstances for banking services were unpropitious, to say the least. The break-up of Yugoslavia had led to the confiscation of foreign currency deposits and the complete breakdown of trust in banks. In both Bulgaria and Romania, trust in banks was shaken by the crises and downturns in the 1990s, while in Albania, people generally avoided banks in the 1990s, turning instead to disreputable 'pyramid' schemes, with disastrous results (described in a previous chapter) following their inevitable collapse in early-1997.

The situation could not be more different today. Currently, anyone visiting the region will observe a banking system that, on the surface, looks pretty similar to those in Western Europe. Many of the same banks that one sees on the streets of Paris, Vienna, Rome and Athens are also present throughout the region. Television commercials on local channels and billboards in the main cities are dominated by pictures of smiling clients (or actors pretending to be clients) of banks. Competition for new business is fierce across the region and interest rates on loans have come down dramatically in recent years. Most importantly, trust has returned to the system—people are far more comfortable now about putting their money into the banking system, whereas before, their savings would more likely have been hidden away under the mattress.

There is no shortage of banks in the region, and this might be a sign that there is still scope for further consolidation.

Bulgaria and Romania have thirty-two and thirty-one banks respectively, as of end-2008. Bosnia and Herzegovina, Croatia and Serbia also have a large number—thirty-two, thirty-three and thirty-seven respectively (also end-2008). There is now a substantial foreign ownership of the banking sector. Most countries in the region now have majority foreign capital, with the asset shares of foreign-owned banks ranging from 53.22 per cent in FYR Macedonia to 94.04 per cent in Bosnia and Herzegovina (in 2008). Finally, the problem of bad loans has, up to now, been well contained. In parallel with this trend, banking supervision in the region has been strengthened immeasurably over the years. While there are still areas that need attention, the progress in this area has been a key factor behind the restoration of confidence in the sector as a whole.

The growth of intermediation has helped to bring interest rates on lending down to rates that were unimaginable even a few years ago. Note that in most countries there is a significant difference between the rates for domestic currency loans and those in foreign currency. This reflects the fear of banks, particularly those that receive funding in foreign currency from parent banks abroad, that the currency will depreciate and so the return on their loans will have a lower value in terms of the relevant foreign currency (usually the euro). However, this spread has narrowed in most cases in recent years, and banks are now more willing to consider lending in local currency than they were in the past.

Foreign banks now dominate the sector in SEE. Is this a good thing or a bad thing? The advantages of having foreign banks operating in a country are obvious: they bring experience of operating in more advanced countries, they are well capitalised and usually have strong support from the parent bank, and they help to increase the level of skills and banking knowledge among locals, with important demonstration effects that can be replicated elsewhere in the local banking sector. But it is not just that the supply of foreign banks has increased, but also the demand for their services is clearly there among the public. Many people in the region no longer trust local banks and will consider putting their money only in foreign-owned banks. But is there a downside to this foreign penetration? This will be considered in the next section.

Credit growth and its dangers

For businesses and households, obtaining credit in recent years became, if not exactly easy, at least much more of an option than it used to be. One measure of the extent of credit penetration in the economy—the one most commonly used—is the ratio of domestic credit to GDP. In South-Eastern Europe, the figures range from 30.51 per cent in Serbia to 85.97 per cent in Montenegro (at end-2007). Several points should be noted. First, the ratio has risen dramatically in recent years, despite the rapid increase in the denominator (GDP). Second, notwithstanding this increase, it is still relatively low by international standards, and certainly well below the levels prevailing in the EU-15. Third, a breakdown of domestic credit into public and private components shows the growing influence of private sector credit, which now accounts for 55.49 per cent of all credit in the region. And fourth, much of this private sector credit is going to households rather than businesses, and a significant chunk of it in the form of mortgages.

Why did private sector credit to households increase so much? As usual in economics, the explanation relies on demand and supply factors. We have already mentioned the supply forces above—the large influx of foreign capital and intense competition for business. On the demand side, the improving business climate has encouraged firms to think about expanding their business, while the growing prosperity means that households can now contemplate major expenses such as houses, holidays and furniture instead of worrying simply about surviving on a day-to-day basis. Modern theories of consumer behaviour are fully consistent with this pattern, as households foresee better times ahead and try to enjoy now some of the fruits of this benevolent horizon. The effects of this are seen in the large external imbalances that are prevalent across the region, since much of the extra spending goes into imports of goods and services.

Could it all end in tears? The region's banking sector is now extremely reliant on foreign funding from parent banks abroad, and the difficulties that banks in 2009 were facing in their own countries could translate into a lower supply of credit, at higher prices (i.e., interest rates) for their subordinate banks in the region. This effect could have important macroeconomic impacts; foreign lending from banks is a key source of financing for the current account deficits in the region, and if this source were to dry up, it could lead to a disruptive 'correction' of the current account, which in practice would be bound to come with a major downturn of the economy. As argued earlier, this disruption could be particularly severe for those countries that maintain a currency board or hard peg. In fact, a slowdown in lending combined with a more stringent evaluation of creditworthiness could be seen as quite welcome under the present circumstances. Furthermore, foreign banks generally recognise the long-term potential of the region and know that it would be premature and self-defeating to pull out now, losing the market share that they fought hard to obtain in recent years. That is why they have been willing in several cases (notably, in Bosnia and Herzegovina, Romania and Serbia) to commit publicly to maintaining their exposure to their subsidiaries in these countries (see Chapter VII below for more discussion).

Non-bank financial institutions

One area where there is likely to be significant development in the coming years lies in the provision of finance through non-banking sources. So far, the importance of this sector has been limited—on the EBRD transition scores, most countries still have a long way to go before reaching the standards of an advanced market economy. Bulgaria, Croatia and Romania score a straight '3', on the 1 to 4+ index, while the others lag behind. However, there have been important advances in equity markets, leasing, pension funds and fixed income markets, all of which are likely to continue. Stock market capitalisation in Croatia for example was 119.6 per cent of GDP (end-2007), a huge jump over the previous year. Equity markets have also become more important in Bulgaria and Romania, and even in the less advanced countries of the region there is growing acceptance of the concept of equity investment.

Trade

One of the biggest casualties of the break-up of former Yugoslavia and the conflict in the region was the collapse of intra-regional trade. In the early years of the present decade, several studies showed that the degree of trading among the countries of the region was well below what would be expected for countries at that level of economic development and in such close proximity. Also, those countries not yet integrated fully into the EU have faced a number of obstacles in reaching EU markets, even though most goods have had tariff-free access to the EU for many years. As a result, this is one of the areas where sustained and intensive efforts have been made, by the international community as well as the locals, to improve the situation. As of mid-2009, most countries are members of the WTO, with the exception of Bosnia and Herzegovina, Montenegro and Serbia which are all in the process.

Existing trade

How much trade exists currently among the countries of the region? At the outset it is important to distinguish between, on the one side, Bulgaria and Romania, which are now EU members, and the rest of the region, which aspires to EU membership. For both Bulgaria and Romania, the dominant partner is the EU, which accounts for 60.6 per cent and 71.9 per cent of total exports respectively in 2007. Not only do those two countries trade little with each other, but also they do not trade much with other countries in South-Eastern Europe. Instead, trade with the rest of the world is also quite important, more so than in other countries of the region. Both countries have expended trade significantly in recent years, aided by major inflows of foreign investment, but it remains to be seen whether, over the medium term, they will be able to stand the full competitive pressures of the rest of the EU.

Turning to the rest of the region, trade data for several countries in the western Balkans (Bosnia and Herzegovina, Montenegro, and Serbia) are patchy and incomplete, so it is difficult to be sure about how much trade, legitimate or otherwise, is actually going on. According to the best available estimates, more than half of the region's trade flows are with the EU. The degree of orientation towards the EU is particularly marked in Albania, with 80.1 per cent of exports destined for EU countries in 2007. However, trade among the western Balkan countries, although still limited, is growing slowly and this trend is likely to be maintained in the coming years.

One reason sometimes suggested for the relatively low levels of intra-regional trade is the overlap between the countries' main export products. Low-skill manufactured goods dominate exports in most cases, while the share of high-skill and technology goods is of only minor importance. For the whole region, primary products, resource-based products, and low-skill manufactured goods make up more than two-thirds of total exports. Textile products and metals are particularly important in Albania, Montenegro, Bosnia and Herzegovina and Macedonia: the latter two countries have benefited in recent years from major investments by the Mittal steel group, while Montenegro's exports are dominated by produce from the giant aluminium conglomerate KAP, acquired by a subsidiary of Rusal in 2005. Croatia and Serbia have a more diversified export structure, although the shipping industry remains highly important for Croatia.

The new CEFTA—what does it mean?

The phrase 'regional cooperation' has been tossed around liberally in the region, at least since the end of the Kosovo conflict and formation of the Stability Pact for South-Eastern Europe. When it comes to promoting trade, the international community has worked hard to try to make the idea of regional cooperation mean something. Initially, countries in the region were encouraged to sign bilateral free-trade agreements (FTAs). The Stability Pact played a major role in this process and, after a lot of huffing and puffing, all agreements were in place by 2003, as well as several with Kosovo, which was represented by UNMIK. But it had been argued for some time that to have 32 separate agreements made little sense, except as a first step towards a common, region-wide agreement. The idea of a single free-trade area for the region had been around since 2001 but was initially deemed politically unacceptable. From 2003 onwards, however, momentum began to build towards a region-wide agreement for the South-Eastern Europe region, similar to the Central European Free Trade Agreement (CEFTA), of which Bulgaria, Croatia and Romania became the sole members after the accession of a number of Central European countries to the EU in May 2004.

The expanded CEFTA was signed by all Stability Pact countries on 19 December 2006. For Bulgaria and Romania, the signature was symbolic since these countries ceased membership of CEFTA twelve days later. The other countries ratified the agreement during 2007. Of course, the designation of 'central Europe' no longer makes geographical sense, but it remains a useful term because it highlights the continuity with the original CEFTA, which was quite successful in terms of promoting intra-regional trade and preparing countries for the rigours of EU competition within the single market. For South-Eastern Europe, there is also the hope that, as countries in the region cooperate more with each other while at the same time making progress towards EU membership, the possibility of future conflict in the region will disappear.

The economic benefits of free trade are well known. However, whether a region-wide FTA will increase trade flows is an open question. Evidence from other regional FTAs, such as the Baltic Free Trade Agreement (BFTA), suggests that they do. But perhaps a stronger case for regional free-trade agreements can be made on the basis of greater investment flows. Openness to trade and the size of the local market are important determinants of FDI inflows. A regional free-trade agreement can therefore attract new investment. Looking at other FTAs like NAFTA in North America, there has been a significant increase in FDI that can be attributed to the agreement, while FTAs such as MERCOSUR and ASEAN have also had important political 'spillovers'. There is every reason to expect similar benefits to accrue to the CEFTA region. The attractions for investors are obvious—a total GDP of US$90 billion, the potential for further catch-up growth, favourable labour and tax costs, an improving business climate, and long-term prospects of EU membership for all.

Trade barriers

Tariffs are not the main problem for traders in the CEFTA region. The trading regime is liberal and tariff levels are similar to EU levels. But in surveys, traders point to a range of non-tariff barriers and obstacles that hinder their business. Evidence from both the EBRD-World Bank Business Environment and Enterprise Performance Survey (BEEPS) and the World Bank's Doing Business survey highlights this point. The BEEPS shows that transportation and customs and trade regulations are often perceived as moderate or major obstacles. In all South-Eastern European countries except Croatia, the percentage of respondents reporting difficulties is above the average for all transition countries. The Doing Business 2010 survey shows that the costs and in particular the time needed to import or export goods are still well above the level of OECD countries.

The new CEFTA will not have any dramatic immediate effects. Over time, however, one can expect important improvements. Customs duties amongst CEFTA members on industrial products were eliminated by the end of 2008 and agricultural products were scheduled to be abolished by the end of 2010. Also, tariff reductions already agreed upon in bilateral free trade agreements will be accompanied by a simplification and unification of coverage and different timetables. A streamlined single system of rules thus replaces the various differing agreements. Another envisaged benefit of CEFTA is that technical barriers to trade will be reduced through harmonisation of standards and regulation with the EU. By creating a joint forum, CEFTA will help ensure that technical barriers and also sanitary and pseudo-sanitary measures are not barriers for free trade and will be used only when they are really necessary. Finally, a Common Rule of Origin has been introduced, meaning that exporters will be entitled to use imported intermediate goods from other CEFTA countries without losing their preferential tariffs not only to other CEFTA countries but also to the EU, EFTA, and Turkey.

Other issues will be addressed over time. For example, the agreement includes also regulation for competition rules and the role of state aid. In general, it aims at introducing competition rules according to EU standards, preventing (amongst other things) volatile state subsidies. Trade of services, mutual investment, public procurement, and intellectual property will also be addressed over time, although the timetable for contentious issues such as the establishment of transparent and non-discriminatory procurement rules granting 'national treatment' to investors from other countries remains unclear. The institutional set up—a Joint Committee, supported by a secretariat in Brussels—is now functioning as of mid-2009. The EU has committed to helping to establish an efficient arbitration system in case of disputes between Members. In summary, there is every reason to expect that both cross-border trade and movement towards EU standards will continue.

Foreign Direct Investment

Prospects for growth and prosperity in South-Eastern Europe depend crucially on a stable and plentiful supply of investment over the medium-term. As noted in the previous chapter, investment into the region from other countries has grown enormously over the present decade. This final section considers whether these inflows are likely to continue. It also looks critically at what the region is doing to attract investors, in terms of taxes and other incentives, and it discusses whether the required human capital will be available to investors, or whether this will end up being a major constraint on growth.

The importance of foreign investment cannot be overemphasised. The region still has huge investment needs, especially in infrastructure but also in many other sectors of the economy, but no country in South-Eastern Europe can finance this investment solely from domestic sources. The large current account deficits that are prevalent in the region imply a big gap between domestic saving and investment, and this gap must be made up either by running down reserves or attracting capital from abroad, either through borrowing or from sale of assets. The big question is whether the region will remain attractive to foreign investors. In order to answer this, one must consider whether the region has much to offer, and what governments are doing to make it more attractive for investors.

Investment needs—privatisation vs. 'greenfield' investment

Much of the dramatic increase in FDI over the current decade has been related closely to the privatisation process in the region. Recent years have seen a number of important and lucrative privatisations and the supply is diminishing. However, there is still a range of sectors across the region with the possibility for strategic sales in the near future. The energy sector has strong potential, but this is the one sector where plans are most unclear and where the process is likely to take the most time. The tourism sector has obvious importance for Croatia and Montenegro, while there are still important telecom deals to be done in Bosnia and Herzegovina and Serbia. The banking sector across the region is mostly private, with Komercijalna Banka in Serbia and Hrvatska Poštanska Banka in Croatia among the only remaining important banks in the region where the state has a majority stake. Elsewhere, there are still significant shares to be sold in various natural resource and manufacturing companies.

The timetable for this process is often unclear and subject to change. As things stand now, the region can still expect to attract significant amounts of privatisation-related FDI over the coming years, but it is difficult to estimate at this point the likely amounts with any precision. The main sources of uncertainty include the current global credit crunch, which could affect the appetite of, and funding availability for, investors, political uncertainty and changing attitudes to energy privatisation, which could imply a greater wish by the state to retain control of energy assets.

Policies to attract investment

Many factors influence investment and this chapter has summarised prospects for some of the most important factors—macroeconomic stability, quality of the business environment and opportunities for finance and trade. Other exogenous factors such as geography and host market size are also important; in this regard, the gradual creation of a regional free-trade area goes a long way to increasing the size of the domestic market and, other things being equal, making it more attractive to potential investors. But which factors matter most? One authoritative recent study highlights the importance of low unit labour costs, low import tariffs and a liberal foreign exchange regime. In addition, institutional factors are also found to be highly significant in determining non-privatisation investment. It is good to see, therefore, that the messages of this book and others about the importance of structural reform are borne out by a rigorous analysis of the hard statistics.

One common finding of many studies of the determinants of investment is the weak or non-existent impact of tax cuts and special tax breaks. Nevertheless, many governments in the region see tax policy as an important tool to attract foreign investors. Several countries have created Special Economic Zones, with exemptions from various taxes and other tax breaks, despite warnings from the IMF and others of the pernicious effects of these zones, while most countries have at various times cut corporate taxes, and subsequently trumpeted the move as a key component of investment promotion policy. In addition, the flat tax fashion that has seduced a number of central European countries has also hit the region, with some form of flat taxes now in place in Albania, Macedonia, Romania, Montenegro, Serbia, and Bulgaria.

As a result of these changes, taxes on corporate income are now fairly low in the region with a median tax rate of 14 per cent as compared to 17.5 per cent in Central and Eastern Europe and 22 per cent in the Commonwealth of Independent States. Montenegro has the lowest rate at 9 per cent, followed closely by Bulgaria and Serbia, both at 10 per cent. None of these countries has what would be considered high statutory corporate tax rates as compared e.g., to the European Union. However, the *statutory* rate is just one determinant among several of the *effective* tax rates. The reason is that there are important differences in the way that depreciation allowances are calculated, for example, and this can make a big difference to investors' calculations of their likely tax burden. Investors need to be aware before being lured by a teasingly low tax rate.

Turning to the other plank of taxation as a tool of investment promotion—tax incentives—the first point to make is that all South-Eastern Europe countries currently have free zone legislation, with varying degrees of tax relief and other incentives. The incentives typically include tax concessions, tax holidays, profit tax exemptions, customs-free imports and sometimes infrastructure subsidies and exemption of labour taxation. In addition, investment in underdeveloped regions, the employment of certain numbers of local employees, and investment in particular sectors all benefit in some circumstances from tax reductions. Overall, besides depreciation rules, customs duty exemption and the established Special Economic Zones seem to be the most relevant incentives provided to foreign investors.

Human capital

The final, and perhaps most important, consideration for a potential investor is whether he/she will be able to hire suitably qualified people to do the job required. This is an area where the situation is changing fast and opinions vary widely about the quality of human capital in the region. One view is that the level of skills is high relative to other emerging market regions of comparable economic size, and therefore the level of human capital is a key attraction of South-Eastern Europe for foreign investors. A more pessimistic point of view would highlight the decline in the quality of school teaching during the transition, the lack of investment in education and the mass exodus of talented young people, especially from former Yugoslav countries and Albania. So who is right?

In order to answer this question, the analysis draws on one more survey—the World Economic Forum's Global Competitiveness Index 2007–08—and looks at each country's ranking in terms of the quality of higher education and training. The results are somewhat sobering. Out of 131 countries in the survey, the highest ranked South-Eastern European country on this indicator is Croatia at 46th place, followed by Romania at 54th place and Bulgaria at 66th place. The worst performer on this particular index is Albania, at 103rd place. Once again, one must be cautious about interpreting these surveys, interesting though they are, too literally. Many investors have been highly satisfied with the quality of the workforce in the region, and education and training systems are gradually being upgraded. However, these results are a reminder that the region has some way to go if it really wants to compete with the rich countries of the west.

One interesting phenomenon in recent years was the sharp decline in unemployment in a number of countries, notably in Bulgaria and Romania, but also in Croatia and Montenegro. The most startling drop was in Romania, where the rate fell at one point (in 2008) to around 4 per cent of the labour force, although it has since increased as a result of the economic crisis. Not surprisingly, many investors are now complaining that they cannot find the right workers, and the resulting skill shortage is threatening to put a brake on Romania's recent impressive growth performance. It also contributes to macroeconomic problems such as inflation by increasing wage pressures.

One factor underlying this drop in unemployment has been increasing outward migration. This phenomenon was associated in the 1990s more with former Yugoslav countries, especially BH, as well as Albania, but it has become more widespread throughout the region in recent years. The accession of Bulgaria and Romania to the EU in January 2007 has made it much easier for individuals to travel abroad, even though they still face employment restrictions throughout the rest of the EU. In the coming years, the challenge will be to ensure that emigrants have an incentive to return to their home countries. If they do, they are likely to bring back not just savings but also fresh skills and ideas that can be put to use in the local economy. This phenomenon is becoming increasingly apparent in some of the Central European countries, such as Poland. However, those contemplating a return home will want to know that, not only is there a job waiting for them, but also decent housing, schools, medical services and other amenities for family life.

7

EMERGING FROM THE CRISIS

As of end-2009 the global economy was in the thick of a deep financial and economic crisis. All of the world's major economies entered recession during 2008 and there are few signs that it will end any time soon. In the current highly globalised economy, virtually no country is immune from the crisis. But some countries are more vulnerable than others. Many people fear that the achievements of the past decade in South-Eastern Europe are now at risk. Not only will there be deep recessions here also, according to the pessimists, but reform reversals and even social upheaval are on the cards.

Is this view justified? We believe not, and we explain why in this concluding chapter. It is important to understand the channels through which the global crisis is affecting the region in order to assess what can be done to mitigate the harmful effects. So far, the responses both of authorities and of firms and ordinary workers have generally been sensible given the difficult circumstances. The international financial community, both public (IFIs) and private (commercial banks), is also helping in a major way, not just through provision of hard cash but also by voicing confidence in the long-term future of the region. It is for this reason that we believe the positive messages of the book remain valid, even though it will be somewhat difficult to retain the faith in the rocky short term.

Effects of the crisis

The origins of the global financial crisis are generally traced back to the United States and the sharp downturn of the housing market, whose growth was increasingly fuelled by 'sub-prime' mortgage lending, which began in 2007. But by mid-2008 there was little indication that South-Eastern Europe was going to be hit in a major way. The boom in economic activity and credit markets showed no sign of abating. Even when things took a dramatic turn for the worse in the major western economies in autumn 2008—the collapse of Lehman Brothers in September was a defining moment—there were still hopes, and indeed a consensus expectation, that South-Eastern Europe would avoid a recession. Most budgets for 2009, and most international forecasters, still expected positive growth in all countries. In the EBRD *Transition Report*, published in November 2008, a slowdown was expected but growth projections for 2009 were still positive in all countries of the region.

The short-term outlook was transformed in the first few months of 2009 by a barrage of almost daily bad news, both from the global economy (especially from the 'Eurozone', the main export market) and within the region itself. It is instructive to compare the IMF growth projections published in the April 2009 *World Economic Outlook*, with official forecasts (on which each country's budget projections were based) at the end of 2008. To take a few examples, Romania has gone from a projected 2.5 per cent growth in 2009 to *minus* 4.1 per cent. Serbia had hoped for 3.5 per cent growth this year, but the revised budget adopted by the government in April 2009 was based on a 2 per cent contraction, as agreed with the IMF. In some cases, governments have lagged behind in admitting how bad things are, partly under the influence of elections. For example, the Macedonian government officially maintained a robustly optimistic view of the economy's prospects right up to Presidential elections in March 2009; once these were safely in the bag, the government acknowledged that the crisis was affecting Macedonia also.

There are various ways in which the crisis is manifesting itself, both through formal data and at the more anecdotal level from firms and workers. Data for the first few months of 2009 on industrial production and exports made for grim reading. For example, industrial output in February was down on the previous February by nearly 20 per cent in Bulgaria, Montenegro and Serbia, and by smaller but still double-digit amounts nearly everywhere else. The collapse of exports has been even more spectacular—down by more than 44 per cent year-on-year in February in Macedonia, and by around 27 per cent in Bulgaria and Serbia. Data on construction, a key part of the boom in most countries, are somewhat slower to come through but initial indications are of a sharp slowdown, with negative annual growth figures already appearing in Bulgaria and Croatia.

Much of the strong growth in recent years can be attributed to, or at least was facilitated by, the rapid rise in availability of credit from banks and other financial institutions (see Chapter V). But many banks began to rein in their lending once it became clear that the global crisis was going to hit this region also with full force. Lending criteria became much tighter, interest rates started to rise and rolling over debts became more difficult. Several banking systems went through a nervous phase in late-2008 when it appeared that depositors would take fright and withdraw their money en masse. In Serbia, for example, it is estimated that around 15 per cent of the deposit base was withdrawn between October and December. Fortunately, a fully-fledged bank run was avoided, and deposits started to return to the system at the end of the year and in the first months of 2009. However, the era of cheap money in the region appears to be over for the time being.

The crisis has also led to a heightened perception of the risks in the region. In the main, the major credit ratings agencies have avoided over-reacting and the number of sovereign downgrades has been limited. Nevertheless, Romania is now rated below investment grade by both Standard and Poor's and Fitch, which has exacerbated the difficulties the country is facing and has raised the cost of borrowing on international markets. Bulgaria was also downgraded by the same two agencies in late-2008 although it remains above investment grade for the time being. Other indicators of risk, such as the spreads on credit default swaps, rose significantly in late-2008, although their usefulness as an indicator of risk is limited by the relative lack of trade of these instruments.

The combination of declining economies and heightened perceptions of risk has led to a marked slowdown in privatisation and investment. As noted elsewhere in the book, there is still a significant privatisation agenda in several countries, but governments are understandably reluctant to sell assets at the kind of bargain-basement price that would be needed to attract a buyer. In some cases, such as that of the Bor mining complex in Serbia, the government decided in early-2009 to try to sell a minority stake only. In other cases, such as the aluminium complex in Mostar in Bosnia, the sale appears to be blocked indefinitely. Other important deals across the region in telecommunications, energy, shipping and other transport have mostly been put on hold.

A number of high-profile investments are also either delayed or perhaps even abandoned. In March 2009, the US-based real estate company Tishman International Companies announced that it was putting on hold a number of major investment projects in Bulgaria and Romania. Fiat's joint investment with the Serbian government at the famous Zastava car plant, announced with great fanfare in 2008, has also been delayed by some months, reflecting the general worldwide malaise in the car industry. The Czech energy company CEZ and the Norwegian power utility Statkraft have both withdrawn from major projects in the Republika

Srpska in Bosnia and Herzegovina, while HEP is facing major delays in investment projects envisaged in the energy investment plan 2006–2013 in Croatia.

Short-term responses

The crisis has created a pall of gloom over the region, just as it has elsewhere in the world. Output is falling virtually everywhere and unemployment is rising, Investor confidence has been damaged, which threatens to prolong the negative effects of the crisis. At this time, therefore, the responses of the different actors could be crucial in determining how long the crisis will last, and how robust the recovery will be once it begins to take hold.

Responses of individuals

As of mid-2009, the response of ordinary individuals through the region to the crisis has been muted. One of the biggest fears of policy-makers was that there would be widespread, and possibly violent, protests by people angry at job losses and declining living standards. But there has been little sign of this kind of activity to date. In general, people seem to understand that this is a genuinely global crisis, the responsibility for which cannot be put at the door of their own politicians or business people. In countries that had elections in the first half of 2009—Macedonia (presidential), Montenegro (parliamentary) and Albania (parliamentary), the ruling parties have done well and retained power. And in cases where a deeply unpopular measure was contemplated, such as in Serbia where the government was considering the imposition of a 6 per cent 'solidarity' tax that would have affected most people, the government has shown flexibility and withdrawn the proposal before things got out of hand. One reason for the relatively phlegmatic response has been that, as this book has demonstrated, people in the region have endured much worse conditions in living memory.

Responses of firms

Many firms have faced difficult choices as the crisis began to take hold. Should they lay off some staff, or reduce the working hours of existing employees, or perhaps try to cut costs by imposing salary freezes and even reductions? All of these options have been used to some extent. High-profile employers such as US Steel in Serbia have reduced the length of the working week as a temporary measure to keep costs under control. Other companies in the vulnerable metals industries, including Mittal-owned companies in Bosnia, Macedonia and Romania, have implemented similar measures. In general, workers have shown a willingness to accept this type of measure, as the alternative may be a permanent closure and resulting job losses. It is important to remember that many of these major foreign-owned firms have invested heavily in their companies in the region to build up market share; they would therefore be highly reluctant to close down for good, and the fact that many of them choose explicitly temporary measures such as working week reduction suggests they take a more positive view of long-term prospects.

Responses of governments and central banks

In general, the response of governments and central banks throughout the region has been prudent. Policy-makers have come under pressure to 'do something' and most of them have responded with various types of packages. But in reality these have amounted to little more than a sticking plaster approach. Some of the measures have veered towards quasi–protectionist incentives to buy local, contrary to the spirit at least of the various regional free trade initiatives over the years, but there has been no wholesale move towards protectionism.

On the fiscal side, all governments recognise that they are in no position to embark on the type of massive Keynesian fiscal stimulus that we have already seen in the US and (to a lesser extent) in the UK. Given how they are perceived by the markets, countries in South-Eastern Europe would be unable to borrow large amounts of money at reasonable rates. Any return to the high deficits of the past would immediately raise doubts about the long-term solvency of the government, and could lead to self-fulfilling runs on the currency. This is something that government want to avoid at all costs. On the other side, there are inevitable pressures from the crisis from greater spending needs (because of higher social security payments) and lower revenues (because of the declining economy). So far, the right balance is being struck between the two, partly thanks to external support (see below).

There is equally little room for manoeuvre on the monetary side. For years, central banks have fretted about excessive credit growth and possible overheating in the economy, and they have often raised reserve requirements and interest rates to dampen this process. Now that commercial banks are reining in their lending, central banks have responded, both by easing reserve requirements—in Bosnia and Herzegovina, Romania and Serbia—and by lowering reference interest rates—in Romania and Serbia. Inflation is less of an issue across the region than a year ago but it still needs to be monitored carefully in Romania and Serbia, and that limits the room for manoeuvre in these countries. Supervision efforts have also been stepped up and banks are being monitored carefully to see if they are facing particular difficulties. So far, the effects on the banking sector have been muted, and central banks have managed to steer a careful course through the situation.

On the reform side, it is perhaps too early to assess whether the region will want to reverse some of the major reforms that have been implemented over the past decade, especially those in the areas of privatisation, corporate governance, competition and infrastructure. But amidst all the debate about what to do in the crisis, there is very little serious argument for reversing transition. Most people recognise that the problems that the crisis has created for the region cannot be solved or even alleviated by a major stepping up of state control or a restriction of competitive forces. Some reforms may be put on hold for a time, but one can say confidently that there will be no return to the past.

Response of the international community

The crisis has led to a significant increase in the activities of a number of international financial institutions in the region. The institution for which this is most true is undoubtedly the IMF. In recent years, most countries in South-Eastern Europe felt that they had outgrown the need for IMF support, and its associated surveillance. By 2008, only Albania still had a lending programme, and this came to an end in late-2008. Several IMF offices in the region were downsized or closed down. But the crisis has exposed most countries to potentially destabilising financing gaps on the external accounts. In plain language, the region had been living beyond its means for years by borrowing from, or selling off assets to, foreign entities. With this supply of capital drying up rapidly, this raised the possibility of countries not being able to meet their external obligations, which could then result in major depreciations of the currency and/or default. The obvious institution to turn to in such a situation is the IMF.

As of May 2009, both Serbia and Romania have signed multi–year programmes with the IMF. Serbia initially negotiated a precautionary standby arrangement of €500 million but, once the severity of the crisis became clear, this was quickly converted into a longer, €3 billion programme. Romania's *volte-face* on IMF support was more dramatic. Having insisted for a long time that the IMF was surplus to Romania's requirements, the authorities changed their minds in early-2009 and managed to arrange a major package of support of almost €20 billion from the IFI community, of which about €13 billion will come from the IMF, €5 billion from the EU and €1 billion each from the EBRD and World Bank. The Bosnian authorities signed a letter of intent in spring 2009 and a three-year agreement of around €1.5 billion was signed in July 2009. Others are likely to follow, whatever they may say publicly.

Other institutions active in the region—the EBRD, EIB and the World Bank—are also stepping up their support. All three institutions joined forces in February 2009 to declare strong support for the banking sector across the whole transition region, including South-Eastern Europe. The headline figure was €24.5 billion in new funding for banks over the next two years—arguably small in comparison to the potential needs of the sector but an important step none the less. But the support is not just confined to the financial sector. All three institutions are active in infrastructure—helping to build and refurbish roads, railways and power systems—and in the corporate sector to ensure that financing for businesses is still available on reasonable terms.

IFI support is not just about pumping in money; it also involves coordination, information and even a bit of arm-twisting now and again. The crisis has resulted in an innovative and highly useful initiative, known as the 'Vienna Initiative', whereby international institutions such as the EBRD and IMF help to ensure that foreign-owned banks in the region will continue to receive support from their parent banks in western Europe. The key idea is to ensure voluntary buy-in from these banks, in the context of IMF-supported lending programmes to the country. In March 2009, the main foreign banks active in Romania and Serbia committed publicly to maintaining their support for their subsidiaries throughout 2009, recognising that it was very much in their own best interests. A similar pledge was made by the six main foreign-owned banks in Bosnia and Herzegovina in July 2009. Without IFI support, it is unlikely that these banks would have been able to come to such an agreement, and the likelihood of one or more banks jumping ship would have been much higher.

The way ahead

While 2009 proved to be a very difficult year for the region, 2010 is likely to see some improvement, but it will be a while before the region sees the high growth rates of recent years.

Some pessimists believe that the crisis will have serious long-term negative effects on the course of economic development and transition. But in our view, this pessimism is unwarranted. There are good reasons to believe that, once the global crisis is over, South-Eastern Europe is well-placed once again to resume growth and attract major inflows of foreign direct investment. Here are three reasons to support this view.

First, there is still a lot of catching up to do. We have already seen that most countries have a GDP per capita well below the EU average. And we know that developing countries can grow faster than developed ones, provided the right conditions are in place. It is a combination of this fact and the reforms that have been implemented so far that explains why the region has spent the past decade catching up on its richer neighbours further west.

Second, whatever the current difficulties facing the European Union, the future of all South-Eastern European countries is undoubtedly within the EU. It is this fact—increasingly recognised by the international investor community—that makes the region increasingly attractive as a place to do business. The exact date of entry is unknown—it will differ by country and there will be difficulties and delays along the way. But many of the benefits of membership arrive long before the actual joining date, in terms of enhanced financial and technical support, liberalisation of the cross-border movement of goods, services and people, and implementation of laws and regulations in line with European standards.

Third, the crisis may encourage rather than delay reforms. For some countries, this will involve slimming down the size of the public sector. This is the main thrust of the revised budget for 2009 that was passed by the Serbian parliament in May 2009, as a condition for securing the IMF agreement. But other countries will also have to look closely not only at the size of the government, which in most cases is large by international standards, but also at measures to make it easier to set up and expand businesses. What is clear is that there is no great appetite for a serious reversal of previous reforms, much less a return to the command economy.

Concluding remarks

Apart from a brief historical overview of the post-World War II decades, our starting point in this volume was the end of the Cold War, which had since 1945 divided Europe from north to south. For most countries emerging from communism, this point, and the following couple of years, marked the beginning of the transition from the one-party state and the planned economy to democracy and multi–party elections, and to an economy based on market principles and a dominant role for the private sector. But for South-Eastern Europe, or more particularly for most of the former Yugoslavia, transition took a back seat while armed conflict and the violent break-up of the country took place. This was not caused by external actors but rather by indigenous forces. The end of the Cold War resulted in a strategic downgrading of this hitherto strategically important region in East-West relations. As a result, the people of the region had found themselves—perhaps for the first time in their history—on their own, with no external powers trying to impose their will either on the region as a whole, or any part of it.

The legacy of this period is hard to shake off, and it would be foolish to maintain that the story of the 1990s is of historical interest only, with little relevance for today's problems. An understanding of the past is essential for making a clear judgement about prospects for the future. Despite the heavy material damage and considerable human casualties, South-Eastern Europe has recovered rather quickly during the present decade. Dire predictions of armed conflicts in the region continuing for decades proved wide of the mark. Democracy, the rule of law and the market economy are established in the countries of the region, though not everywhere to the same extent. As previously in the former Communist-ruled Central Europe, the prospect of EU membership, however distant, acted a spur to internal political and economic reforms and better intra-regional relations.

A renewed war in the region has become almost unthinkable. This is not least because powerful lobbies have a strong vested interest in regional concord rather than, as so often before, conflict. Good political relations between the individual countries of the region are now matched by rapidly expanding business cooperation and joint intra-regional infrastructure projects in transport, energy, environment and other spheres, backed by the support of financial institutions such as the EBRD, the EIB, the World Bank and other international bodies. Even in cases of continuing political disputes such as between Skopje and Athens over the Macedonian name, economic relations and investment flourish. All of these points mean that South-Eastern Europe is slowly but surely turning into a zone of cooperation and integration with the rest of Europe and the world.

What will the region look like in ten years time (i.e., in 2019)? Given the countries' collective capacity to surprise us, it is wise to be cautious about making predictions. However, some things are more likely to happen than others. On the political side, there is a very good chance that all countries will be full members of the European Union by then. This is the one thing that binds together competing interests and around which politicians and ordinary people can unite. Of course it will require that the EU itself gets its act together, something which is in doubt after the delays in ratifying and implementing the Lisbon Treaty.

Notwithstanding the present uncertainty, one can expect to see further catch-up on central Europe over the next ten years. South-Eastern Europe has the advantage for potential investors of significantly lower wages and, for the time being, plenty of opportunities for profitable investments. This includes investments into key state-owned sectors, where the privatisation programme is not yet complete. As economies continue to grow, there is likely to be a significant return of emigrants, which will help to alleviate the labour supply shortages that have arisen in recent years in countries such as Bulgaria and Romania. One requirement for the region to prosper is further major investment into infrastructure, which is essential for facilitating trade, investment and tourism. This is an area where the state, international institutions and the private sector need to cooperate in order to achieve the best results. Already, we have seen how this cooperation can bring fruitful results in selected areas, but there is scope for much more to be done.

Will South-Eastern Europe become just like Western Europe? It would be more realistic to ask whether it can be like Central European countries such as Hungary, Poland and the Czech and Slovak Republics. There are obvious parallels between South-Eastern Europe now and some of these central European countries five or ten years ago, in terms of the level of economic development and the strength of market forces and reforms. However, each country has its own path and potential. The conditions are now in place for this potential to be achieved, but ultimately it will be up to politicians and, increasingly, businesses and entrepreneurs to make sure this happens.

BIBLIOGRAPHY

(This short note does not offer an extensive bibliography on the subject of this book but, rather, points to a relatively small number of works that the authors thought, without necessarily endorsing fully, the interested reader might find interesting and helpful.)

General works

Margaret Macmillan's *Peacemakers. The Paris Conference of 1919 and Its Attempt to End War (London:* John Murray, 2001) is an essential as well as a highly readable account of the political context within which the new, post-1918 Europe was shaped in the aftermath of the First World War. Richard Crampton's *Eastern Europe in the Twentieth Century.* (London: Routledge 1997. Second Edition) is an informative and reliable historical survey of the region from the Baltic to the Adriatic, taking the reader right up to and beyond the 1989–91 revolutions. The same author's *The Balkans since The Second World War* (London and New York: Longman, 2002) is an authoritative, up-to-date account taking in Albania, Bulgaria, Greece, Romania and former Yugoslavia and its successor-states. Despite having been published nearly 40 years ago, Paul Lendvai's *Eagles into Cobwebs* (London: Macdonald, 1970) is still valid for its acute and perceptive analysis of the relationship between communism and nationalism in South-Eastern Europe. *The Other Balkan Wars* (Washington: Carnegie Endowment, 2003) is a reprint of the famous Carnegie Endowment Inquiry into the Balkan wars in 1912 and 1913, with a new introduction and reflections on the 1990s conflict by

IN SEARCH OF THE BALKAN RECOVERY

George F. Kennan. *Transition: the First Decade* (Cambridge., Mass. and London: MIT Press, 2001) edited by Mario I. Blejer and Marko Škreb is a close analysis, by a number of top world specialists, of the first decade of economic and social transition in the whole post-Communist region. Much of the analysis in Chapters V and VI of this book draws on the annual EBRD *Transition Report* (various issues). The 2007 edition of the *Transition Report* focuses on the EBRD/World Bank Life in Transition Survey (LiTS). For more on the LiTS, see *Life in Transition: A Survey of People's Experiences and Attitudes* (EBRD, 2007). Valuable cross-country analysis and data are published regularly by various institutions, including the IMF, the World Bank and the Vienna Institute for International Economics.

Albania

The post-1945 'Albanian Way' is authoritatively analysed in Bernard Tönnes's *Sonderfall Albanien. Enver Hoxha's 'eigener Weg' und die historischen Urspunge seiner Ideologie* (München: Oldenbourg 1980). *Albania: From Anarchy to Balkan Identity* (New York: New York University Press, 1997) by Miranda Vickers and James Pettifer covers the first decade of political transition. Paulin Kola's *The Search for Greater Albania* (London: Hurst, 2003) analyses the myths and the reality surrounding the claims about Greater Albanian expansionism. *Albania and the European Union: the Tumultuous Journey Towards Accession and Integration* by Mirela Bogdani and John Loughlin (London: I.B. Tauris, 2007) traces Albania's slow but steady process of Europeanisation. In *The Accursed Mountains. Journeys in Albania* (London: Flamingo, 1999), Robert Carver offers a vivid portrait of the country in the early stages of transition. *Albania in Crisis: the Predictable Fall of the Shining Star* by Daniel Vaughan-Whitehead (Northampton, MA: Elgar, 1999) analyses economic developments in the run-up to pyramid scheme crisis of 1997.

Bulgaria

A Concise History of Bulgaria (Cambridge:Cambridge University Press, 1997. Second, updated edition 2005) is by the leading British historian of Bulgaria, Richard Crampton. The most up-to-date information is to be found in his *Bulgaria*, published as a paperback by the Oxford University Press in 2008. The economic background is covered in John A. Bristow's *The Bulgarian Economy in Transition, Studies in Communism im Transition* (Cheltenham and Brookfield, Vt.: Edward Elgar, 1996) and in Iliana Zloch-Christy's *Bulgaria in a Time of Change: Economic and Political Dimensiona* (Aldershot and Brookfield, Vt.: Avebury, 1996).

Romania

Martyn Rady's *Romania in Turmoil: A Contenporary History* (London: I.B. Tauris, 1992) provides a useful background to the post-1945 period and the eventual collapse of the Communist regime. *Post-Communist Romania. Coming to Terms with Transition* (Houndsmill: Palgrave, 2001), edited by Duncan Light and David Phinnmore, analyses various aspects of transition. The pre-transition period is treated in David Turnock's *The Romanian Economy in the Twentieth Century* (London: Croom Helm, 1986). Gilbert Trond's *Nationalism and Communism in Romania: the Rise and Fall of Ceauşescu's Personal Dictatorship* (Boulder, Colorado: Westview Press, 1991) traces the career of the politician who successfully harnessed nationalism to his regime's purposes. The still hugely controversial issue of the role of the secret police in Communist Romania is the subject of Dennis Deletant's *Ceauşescu and the Securitate* (London, Hurst, 1996).

Former Yugoslavia

A key work for the understanding of Yugoslavia's main political problems is Ivo Banac's *The National Question in Yugoslavia: origins, history, politics* (Ithaca: Cornell University Press, 1984). In *Great Britain and the Creation of Yugoslavia. Negotiating Balkan Nationality and Identity* (London and New York: Tauris Academic Studies, 2008) James Evans analyses the circumstances in which the muddled, historically unfounded concept of a single 'Yugoslav' nation made up of three 'tribes' became accepted by one of the main powers responsible for the shaping of post-1918 South-Eastern Europe.

IN SEARCH OF THE BALKAN RECOVERY

An indispensable, up-to-date volume by leading scholars from the region as well as from the West, providing full background to, and the political, economic and social impact of, the violent break-up of Yugoslavia and of its aftermath, is *Der Jugoslawien-Krieg. Handbuch zu Vorgeschichte, Verlauf und Konsequenzen* (Wiesbaden: Verlag für Sozialwissenschaft, 2007. Second Edition) edited by Dunja Melčić, a respected Frankfurt-based academic specialist on the region. Veteran American 'Yugoslavist' Lenard J. Cohen is joint author, with Jasna Dragović-Soso, of *State Collapse in South-Eastern Europe. New Perspectives on Yugoslavia's Disintegration* (Fort Wayne, Indiana: Purdue University Press, 2008). British academic John B. Allcock's *Explaining Yugoslavia* (London: Hurst, 2000) adopts the socio-economic approach to the analysis of the country's problems leading to its ultimate disintegration. Dejan Jović's *Jugoslavija—država koja je odumrla 1974–1990. (The State that Withered Away 1974–1990)*, published simultaneously in 2003 by Prometej in Zagreb and Samizdat B92 in Belgrade, is a thoughtful, well-researched scholarly work setting Yugoslavia's collapse within the context of the ideological and political debates and disagreements within its political elite. Slavko Goldstein's award-winning study entitled *1941. Godina koja se vraća (1941.The Year Which Returns)*, published by Novi liber in Zagreb in 2007, is an important contribution to the understanding of the background to post-1945 Tito Yugoslavia's political problems and tensions. Two authoritative works dealing with the war in Croatia sparked off by the rebellion in 1990 of a part of the local Serb minority population are *Srpska pobuna u Hrvatskoj (The Serb Rebellion in Croatia)* by Nikica Barić (Zagreb: Golden Marketing-Tehnička knjiga, 2005); and *Goli život. Socijalna dimenzija pobune Srba (Naked Life. The Social Dimension of the Serb Rebellion)* by Ozren Žunec (Zagreb: Demetra, 2006).

The Serbian case against Tito's Yugoslavia is summed up in the seminal 1986 *Memorandum* prepared under the auspices of the Serbian Academy of Sciences in Belgrade by a group of scholars and prematurely leaked to the press. The full text was first published in the Zagreb journal *Naše teme* (1989, 33 (1–2, pp. 128–163). For a detailed critical anlysis, see *Antimemorandum* by Miroslav Brandt, a Croat historian, in *Izvori velikosrpske agres-*

BIBLIOGRAPHY

ije, edited by Bože Čović and published jointly in Zagreb in 1991 by the publishing houses August Cesarec and Školska knjiga. A Serb answer to the critics is to be found in *Memorandum SANU. Odgovor na kritike* by Kosta Mihailović and Vasilije Krestić (Beograd: SANU, 1995). In *Tuđman. Biografija* (Zagreb: Profil, 2004) Darko Hudelist provides a well-documented, critical political portrait of independent Croatia's first leader Behind-the-scenes Croat-Serb contacts during the armed conflict are covered by Hrvoje Šarinić, a senior Croat figure close to President Franjo Tuđman in *Svi moji tajni pregovori sa Slobodanom Miloševićem 1993–95 (98) (All My Secret Talks with Slobodan Milošević)* published by Globus in Zagreb in 1999. Borisav Jović, a senior political figure and close Milošević ally within the Serbian party elite provides insight into Serbian aims and motives in his diary *Poslednji dani SFRJ.* (Beograd, Politika, 1995). The best biography of Milošević to date is *Slobodan Milošević and the Destruction of Yugoslavia* (Durham and London: Duke University Press, 2002) by Louis Sell, a former American diplomat. *Serbia under Milošević. Politics in the 1990s* (London: Hurst, 1999) by Robert Thomas covers in detail Serbian internal politics during the period of the 'Wars of Yugoslav Succession'. Jasna Dragovic-Soso deals with the political role played by the Serb intelligentsia in *Saviours of the Nation* (London, Hurst, 2002).
The background to the still lingering controversy about the role of Germany at the start of the armed conflict in the former Yugoslavia is critically covered in *Limits of Persuasion. Germany and the Yugoslav Crisis, 1991–1992* by Michael Libal, a senior German diplomat (Westport, Connecticut and London: Praeger, 1997). Western (particularly British) policy towards the conflict in Bosnia is critically examined in Brendan Simms's *Unfinest Hour: Britain and the Destruction of Bosnia* (London: Allen Lane, 2001). A detailed analysis of the war in Bosnia is to be found in *How Bosnia Armed. From Milošević to Bin Laden* by British academic Marko Attila Hoare (London: Saqi, 2004) and also in *Genocide in Bosnia* (College Station, Texas:Texas AM University Press, 1995) by American academic Norman Cigar. Elizabeth Roberts's *A Realm of the Black Mountain. A History of Montenegro* (London: Hurst, 2006) brings the story right up to date.

So does Kenneth Morrison's *Montenegro: A Modern History*, published by I.B. Tauris in 2009.

James Pettifer's *The New Macedonian Question (Basingstoke: Macmillan, 1999)* places the independent state's problems in a geopolitical context. The Macedonian question is also treated in *Macedonia. Warlords and Rebels in the* Balkans by John Phillips (New Haven and London: Yale University Press, 2004). Noel Malcolm's *Kosovo: A Short History* (London: Macmillan, 1998) is the first ever, full-length history by a British academic of Kosovo's history. *Kosovo/Kosova. Mythen. Daten. Fakten* by Wolfgang Petritsch, Karl Kaser and Robert Pichler (Klagenfurt-Wien-Ljubljana-Tuzla-Sarajevo: Wieser *Verlag*, 2004) combines history with expert, up-to-the-date analysis of current events. *Slovenia and the Slovenes. A Small State and the New Europe* (London: Hurst, 2000) by James Gow and Cathie Carmichael is a useful introduction, combining history and current issues. *Slovenia 1945. Memories of Death and Survival after World War II* (London: I.B. Tauris, 2005) by John Corsellis and Marcus Ferrar deals with the bloody and still politically highly controversial aftermath of the civil war in Slovenia during the Second World War.

INDEX

Ahtisaari, Martti: Plan for Kosovo,
86–7; UN special envoy, 84–5
Albania, 12–13, 32, 92, 112–13,
125, 133, 146, 148, 154, 157,
191; abolition of religion (1967),
14; and China, 14, 126; and
Greece, 15, 17; and IC, 172; and
IMF, 194; and Kosovo, 9; and
SAA, 116; and USA, 17; Communist Party of (PKS), 10, 16–17,
50; constitutional reformation
(1991), 15; corruption problem,
170; Democratic Party of (PDS),
16, 49, 52; economy of, 129–30,
139–40, 142, 144, 165, 171,
178; emigrating population, 185;
financial crisis (1997), 50, 131–2,
173; integration of Kosovo into
Yugoslavia (1945), 10; invitation
from NATO (2008), 120; joining
of Tripartite Pact (1941), 18;
member of WTO, 150; resources
of, 13; Soviet bloc, 7, 13; Socialist Party of (PSS), 50; support for
Kosovo's declaration of independence (2008), 52; taxation system
of, 184; transition to democracy,
3, 49; unemployment level, 186
Alia, Ramiz: reforms of, 15
Antonescu, General Ion: death of
(1953), 23–4; overthrow of, 23;
trial of (1946), 23

Badinter, Robert: report of, 101–2
Baker, James: US Secretary of State,
93
Băsescu, Traian: and Boc, Emil, 60;
electoral success of, 59; leader of
PD, 59
Balli Kombëtar (BK): and KPJ, 9;
support for German intervention
(1943), 10
Baltic Free Trade Agreement
(BFTA), 180
Berov, Liuben: government of, 22
Bersha, Sali: electoral defeat and
resignation of (1997), 50; electoral success (2005), 51; leader
of PDS, 16, 49, 51–2; policies of,
51–2; support for Kosovo, 52
Boc, Emil: and Băsescu, Traian,
60; background of, 60; leader
of PDL, 60; prime minister of
Romania, 60
Boris III, King, 17–18
Bosnia and Herzegovina, ix, 29,
112–13, 115, 146, 148, 154, 194;
and IC, 172; and NATO, 17; and
SAA, 116–17; arms industry of,
104, 128; corruption problem,
170; Croat Defence Council
(HVO), 44–5; currency board,
141, 166; economy of, 127–8,
136, 138–9, 144, 155, 164, 171,
174, 176, 178, 190, 192–3, 195;

INDEX

Steering Group (ISG), 90; Lisbon Treaty, 198; Maastricht Treaty (1992), 162–3, 167; members of, x, 2–5, 61, 111, 125, 140, 161, 179–80, 198; prospective members of, x, 27, 197; recognition of Bosnia and Herzegovina (1992), 108; recognition of Kosovo's independence (2008), 118; Stabilisation and Association Agreement (SAA), 86–7, 89, 116, 118; Stabilisation and Association Programme (SAP), 115–17; recognition of former Yugoslav republics, 104

Fino, Bashkim: government of, 50
First World War, 28; and Bulgaria, 9, 18; and Montenegro, 34
France, 84, 89, 91, 95, 99; and Dayton Peace Accords, 111; member of 'Contact' Group, 66, 109; recognition of Croatia and Slovenia, 104–5; rejection of EU Constitutional Treaty (2005), 119

Generalised Agreement on Trade and Tariffs (GATT): and Romania, 26
Geoană, Mircea: electoral success of, 60; Romanian ambassador to USA, 60
Germany, 8; and Second World War, 15, 17–18; and Serbia, 106; collapse of Berlin Wall (1989), 4, 7, 91; Constitution of (1949), 107; Federal Republic of (FRG), 91; foreign interests of, 106; German Democratic Republic (GDR), 91; member of 'Contact' Group, 66, 109; Nuremburg Trials, 46; pressure for recognition of Croatia and Slovenia, 105–7; Stability Pact for South East Europe (SP), 4, 112–13, 134, 179

Gheorghiu-Dej, Gheorge: death of (1965), 25; leader of Romanian Communist Party, 25
Gligorov, Kiro: president of Macedonia, 47
Gorbachev, Mikhail, 102–3
Gračanin, Petar: order for Slovenian border confrontation (1991), 41
Greece, 3: and Albania, 15, 17; and Macedonia, 47–8, 118, 128, 130, 132; Civil War, 10–11; Communist Party of, 17; Western influence in, 7
Gregurić, Franjo: prime minister of Croatia, 70

Habsburg Empire: collapse of, 28
Holbrooke, Richard: envoy of Clinton, Bill, 46, 65
Hoxha, Enver: abolition of religion in Albania (1967), 14; death of (1985), 15; leader of PKS, 10; rivalry with Xoxe, Koçi, 13; support for Stalin, Joseph, 13
Hungary, 12, 112, 199; economy of, 129; influences on, 7; Revolution (1956), 12, 25
Hurd, Douglas, 93

Iliescu, Ion, 60; electoral success of, 58
Information Bureau of Communist and Workers' Parties (Cominform): expulsion of KPJ (1948), 7–8, 10, 20, 30, 94; USSR control of, 7
International Criminal Tribunal for the Former Yugoslavia (ICTY), 71, 86, 89, 115, 118; created at The Hague by UN, 46; extradition of Milošević, Slobodan, 77; trial of Gotovina, General Ante, 71; trial of Karadžić, Radovan, 89, 119
International Monetary Fund (IMF), 156, 161; and Albania,

INDEX

INDEX

Refugees (UNHCR), 68; Implementation Force (IFOR), 47; Interim Administration Mission in Kosovo (UNMIK), 68, 83, 179; members of, 108; Office of the Special Envoy for Kosovo (UNOSEK), 84; peacekeepers, 109; Protected Areas (UNPAs), 42, 101; Protections Force (UNPROFOR), 101, 109; Security Council, 46, 65, 84–5, 101, 119; sponsor of Southeast European Cooperation Initiative (SECI), 112
United States of America (USA), 2, 40, 111–12, 120; and Albania, 17; and Romania, 26; and NATO, 120; Central Intelligence Agency (CIA), 28; effect of Cold War, 107; First Gulf War, 102, 107; fiscal stimulus, 192; foreign economic investments, 192; International Steering Group (ISG), 90; member of 'Contact' Group, 66, 109; recognition of Kosovo's independence (2008), 120; role in global financial crisis (2007–9), 188

Văcăriou, Nicolae: prime minister of Romania, 27
Vance-Owen plan, 44, 100
Vasile, Radu: failure of government of, 58; prime minister of Romania, 58
Videnov, Zhan: and murder of Lukanov, Andrei, 53; electoral success of (1994), 53; resignation of (1996), 53

World Bank (WB), 111, 113, 124, 194–5, 198; Business Environment and Enterprise Performance Survey (BEEPS), 169–71, 180; 'Doing Business' database, 171,

180; Life and Transition Survey (2006), 137, 153, 155, 162
World Economic Forum: Global Competitiveness Index, 185
World Trade Organisation (WTO): and Bosnia and Herzegovina, 177; and Montenegro, 177; and Serbia, 177; members of, 150, 177

Xoxe, Koçi: and PKS, 10; support for KPJ, 10; rivalry with Hoxha, Enver, 13

Yugoslavia, 30, 123, 133, 197; and SAA, 116, 154, 156; Communist Party of (KPJ), 7–10, 17, 20, 29; Constitution of (1974), 31–2, 97; economic sanctions against (1992), 62, 64, 109, 128; economic strength of, 125–6, 132; Federal Republic of (FRY), ix, 61–2, 64, 109, 112, 116, 130, 134; foreign debt of, 127; formerly Kingdom of Serbs, Croats and Slovenes, 8; influences on, 7; integration of Kosovo (1945), 10; League of Communists of (SKJ), 29, 31, 68; transition to democracy, 3; Western interest in, 11; Yugoslav People's Army (JNA), 31, 37, 39–44, 92, 96–7, 101, 103–4
Yugolsav Wars, ix, 1; legacy of, 50; outbreak of, 96

Zemun Clan: crackdown on in Operation Sabre (2003), 78; link to Red Beret, 78
Zhivkov, Todor: deposed (1989), 21; failed policies of, 21
Živković, Zoran: call for general election (2003), 79; Operation Sabre (2003), 77–8; prime minister of Serbia, 77

215